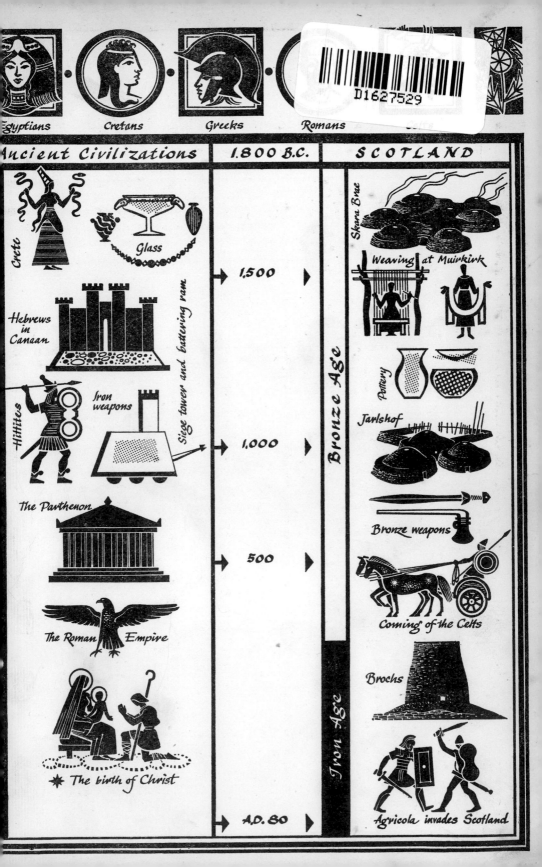

Egyptians   Cretans   Greeks   Romans

Ancient Civilizations | 1,800 B.C. | SCOTLAND

Crete

Glass

Hebrews in Canaan

Hittites

Iron weapons

Siege tower and battering ram

The Parthenon

The Roman Empire

The birth of Christ

1,500

1,000

500

A.D. 80

Bronze Age

Iron Age

Skara Brae

Weaving at Muirkirk

Pottery

Jarlshof

Bronze weapons

Coming of the Celts

Brochs

Agricola invades Scotland

HISTORY FOR YOUNG SCOTS
BOOK ONE

AT SKARA BRAE (*See page 14*)

HISTORY FOR
YOUNG SCOTS

by

A. D. CAMERON

Principal Teacher of History
Inverness Royal Academy

BOOK ONE

From the Earliest Times
to the Union of 1707

With Illustrations by
JOHN DUGAN

OLIVER AND BOYD
EDINBURGH AND LONDON

OLIVER AND BOYD LIMITED
Tweeddale Court, Edinburgh 1
39A Welbeck Street, London W.1

SBN 05 000067 5

FIRST PUBLISHED 1963
THIRD IMPRESSION 1968

Printed in Great Britain by
Oliver and Boyd Ltd., Edinburgh

PREFACE

Following the introduction of the Ordinary Grade examination, teachers have been faced with the problem of what history should be taught in the first two years of the Senior Secondary School. The two books in this series, which form a complete course from earliest times to the present day, are designed to provide an answer.

The guiding principle has been to select those facts that children ought to know about the history of their own country and its place in the world down the centuries. Chapters such as *The Roman Soldiers at Newstead* and *Life in the Burghs in the Seventeenth Century* are presented as examples of life in Scotland at particular times, while much of the traditional English history taught in some Scottish schools has been omitted: the Wars of the Roses and Henry VIII's wives are not, after all, part of the Scottish heritage.

To help children to see that a history book is only the beginning and not the whole story, the exercises are intentionally practical. In some, pupils are encouraged to find out more about events in other countries, and in others hints are given to help them to discover their own local history.

Help given by many librarians and friends, especially Miss A. S. Henshall and Mr. Stuart Maxwell of the National Museum of Antiquities who read the prehistoric and medieval chapters, is gratefully acknowledged.

A. D. CAMERON

ACKNOWLEDGMENTS

For kind permission to include excerpts from copyright material, the author and publishers of this book offer their thanks to the following:

Messrs. Constable & Co. Ltd., for the translation on page 43 of a verse by an Irish scribe, from *Ancient Irish Poetry* by the late Kuno Meyer; Messrs. Hodder & Stoughton Ltd. and the author, for the translation on page 47 of a similar verse, from *Celtic Sunrise* by Diana Leatham; The Edinburgh University Press and the author, for the translation on page 61 of a passage from the Old French romance *Fergus*, from *The Normans in Scotland* by R. L. G. Ritchie; Messrs. Thomas Nelson & Sons Ltd., for the translation on page 95 of a passage from the *Declaration of Arbroath*, from *Supra Crepidam* by the late Lord Cooper; Sir Alexander Gray, for the quotation on page 97 from his poem *Scotland*; and Mrs. W. H. Ogilvie, for the quotation on page 130 from *Ho! For the Blades of Harden* by the late Will H. Ogilvie.

CONTENTS

Chapter 1

PEOPLE AND THEIR NEEDS

There are more than five million of us in Scotland to-day, living mainly in towns. While some of the towns are as far apart as Thurso and Dumfries, or Oban and Aberdeen, most of them are in the central Lowlands, between the Highlands of the north and the Uplands of the south. They have grown up in central Scotland, many in the last two centuries, because of the coal underneath them.

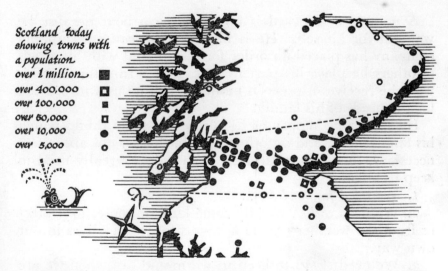

Scotland today
showing towns with
a population
over 1 million ■
over 400,000 ◻
over 100,000 ■
over 50,000 ◻
over 10,000 ●
over 5,000 ○

Most of you attend town schools. Your fathers and elder brothers and sisters work in factories, workshops, shipyards, or mines, *producing* things; or drive lorries or vans, *transporting* things from place to place, or in offices and shops, taking orders and *selling* things. All these jobs are connected, and are necessary to support our modern lives.

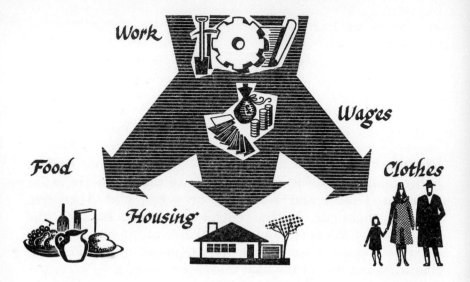

A man in a shipyard is not building a boat because he wants it for himself. He is busy there because a shipping company has placed an order for a ship, and with hundreds of others he plays his part in making it. In return for his work he receives a wage in money which he uses to provide for the needs of his family.

He spends his money as he pleases on some things which his family need, and on others which, though not absolutely necessary, they happen to like. What do we really need to keep us alive?

1. We need *food and drink*.

2. We need *shelter*, usually some kind of house, to protect us from the weather and to allow us to live our lives in our own way.

3. We need *clothes* to keep us warm and dry when we are out in the open.

Probably you can think of many other things which you feel you need, but these three, food, shelter, and clothing, are our basic or *economic* needs. Without them we could not live.

In the countryside the farm worker helps to grow food,

but not all the different foods which he likes to eat. He lives in a house which he did not build and wears clothes which he did not make.

To-day, working at one job, earning a wage, and spending it in his own way, a man can keep himself alive without growing all his own food, building his own house or making his own clothes.

It was not always so.

In early Scotland

Imagine yourself on a deserted island. You are between the sea and the unexplored forest. You begin to feel hungry and think about food. You must look for it. You are in the same position as the earliest man in Scotland. He was a food-gatherer. He had most chance of survival on the seashore, where he gathered shellfish. At the right seasons some bushes yielded berries, and in the forest he collected nuts.

To get food at other times, he learned to fish and hunt. He caught fish with his hands, or by stunning them with a stone, or by spearing them with a harpoon made of bone or antler. He tied a cord to his harpoon to prevent it being carried away downstream. He might be lucky enough to find, washed up on the beach, a whale from which he hacked off flesh with a bone mattock. Except on the windswept north mainland and islands, Scotland was covered by trees. Animals abounded, giant deer, elk, wild oxen, wolves, beavers, lemmings, wild cats, mountain hares, boars, ponies, and brown bears. Man learned to make weapons for hunting. Often he was not as strong as the animals he hunted, and he went hunting with other men. Together they made pits to trap animals.

After people discovered how to make fire they no longer had to eat fish or meat raw. If you strike a piece of flint on a stone you make sparks, and if you use dried moss or fungus or rotten wood or thistle-down as tinder, it will smoulder and burst into flame. You have then made a fire with a 'strike-a-light'. Another way of making a fire was by rubbing wood against wood in the Boy Scout manner.

A piece of wood with grooves in it was placed on the ground and a round piece of wood was rubbed vigorously in a groove until the friction made dust and the heat caused the dust to smoulder and catch fire.

The discovery of fire completely altered the life of man. People could keep themselves warm, cook their food, and ward off wild animals at night. Later they learned to work metals and make weapons by the heat of a fire.

After scraping the skins of animals on the inside with a sharp stone, they sewed them into clothes. By rubbing bones down, they made needles for sewing and harpoons for hunting and fishing.

Where there were caves they sheltered in them. In most places they probably lived in tents of skins, the first man-made homes in Scotland.

Of these tent-like dwellings nothing remains, but they are the kind of homes we should expect a hunting people to use (compare the tepees of Red Indians). The only traces these people have left are solid things like stone, bone, and pottery made of fired clay. Later people have left metal tools and weapons. Wood, bark, leather, and later cloth, must have been just as important in the daily lives of early peoples. From bark alone they could have made baskets and boxes, cradles, shoes, torches, handles for tools, and roofs for houses. No traces of these remain to tell us the full story of the people who used them.

Something for You to Do

1. (a) Is your town marked on the map?
   (b) What is its name?
   (c) How many people live in it?
2. The number of people living in Glasgow, Edinburgh, Aberdeen, Dundee, and Paisley adds up to two million. What fraction of the population of Scotland lives in these five towns?
3. What do most people work at in your town?
4. Name the three groups in the second paragraph of this chapter into which most jobs are divided. In which group does your father's, or brother's or uncle's job belong?
5. Food, shelter, and clothing are necessary to keep us alive. What other things do you feel you need to make life enjoyable?
6. (a) What kinds of edible berries and nuts grow wild to-day?
   (b) Which animals run wild in the countryside now?
7. (a) What different methods of 'striking a light' are used to-day?
   (b) Which peoples at the present day use the old methods?
   (c) Write a paragraph on 'Fire is a good servant but a bad master'.
8. On a double page of your notebook start off a chart with the headings given below:

		People	Food	Shelter	Clothing
1		Early Man			

Fill in the blanks showing how early man satisfied his needs. As you read the coming chapters you can add information about later peoples.

Chapter 2

THE FIRST FARMERS

It was in the Near East that men first made so much progress that they could be considered civilised. Before 3500 B.C. good crops of grain and flax were being raised on the mud-flats of the Niledel ta in Egypt. Farther up the river, trenches were cut to carry water to the fields. When the ox-drawn plough was introduced it became possible to grow much more food with considerably less labour. Egypt became prosperous under the rule of kings called *Pharaohs*. The royal officials collected taxes and enforced the laws. They commanded a huge force of labourers who worked on the control of the River Nile and the construction of canals, public buildings, and tombs. The Great Pyramid, for example, built as a royal tomb, is thought to have taken a hundred thousand men about twenty years to build.

At about the same time, settlers were attracted to Mesopotamia, the land between the two great rivers, Tigris and Euphrates, which flow into the Persian Gulf. In addition to cultivating the soil, people kept cows for milk and made cloth from the wool of their sheep. Before 2500 B.C. their rulers had well-equipped and disciplined soldiers, some of whom charged into battle in chariots. When silver money was introduced, buying and selling replaced the exchange of goods. The value of the money depended on its weight. Other metals, including gold and copper, were fashioned into beautiful ornaments by skilful smiths.

In both Egypt and Mesopotamia people could write. In Egypt they wrote on paper which they made from strips of river reed called papyrus, and in Mesopotamia they cut out the letters on tablets of wet clay. Both civilisations produced a calendar, showing knowledge of the measurement of time.

The Egyptian calendar was the more accurate, dividing the year into twelve months of thirty days each, with five feast days at the end to make a total of 365 days. In these ways the peoples of the Near East were further advanced than those in Europe.

New Stone Age Men in Scotland

About 2500 B.C. new people came to settle in Scotland. They came from the shores of south-west Europe in boats hollowed out of tree trunks. They came gradually, hugging the coast, some settling in the south and east of England. Many perished on the way, but the most skilful and the strongest survived. By way of the Irish Sea they reached and settled on the western mainland and islands, while some ventured farther north to settle in the Shetland Isles. The east coast was settled too, when the descendants of the people who had made their homes in south-east England came north by sea. We do not know what race of men they were, because they left no written records, but we know their way of life from the materials they used for the best of their weapons, and we call them New Stone Age men.

These people were better equipped to obtain their basic needs than the earlier food-gatherers and primitive hunters had been. They had tamed dogs to help them in hunting. They had weapons of polished stone, shaped and smoothed. Their cutting and boring tools, however, were not like modern tools, because they did not know about the use of metals. If you look at the time chart at the front of this book, you will see that before 2000 B.C. some peoples were already using copper. In Scotland, however, men were still using

HOW THE NEW STONE AGE MEN CAME •

lumps of hard stone called flint, which could be split into flakes.

Knives, borers, scrapers, daggers, and arrowheads were fashioned out of flakes and sharpened by being struck on the edge with a hammer stone. Among the weapons used were the bow and arrow. The shaft of the arrow was shaved smooth with a flint knife and scraper, the tail was trimmed with feathers from the eagle or the goose, and in the head a piece of flint was fixed. The earliest arrowheads were shaped like a birch or a willow leaf.

If you think that stone tools were not of much use you are wrong. Not long ago a worker in Denmark was given stone tools instead of steel ones. He cut wood, made planks, and built a complete house with them by himself in less than twelve weeks.

Living at Skara Brae

Let us take a close-up view of the New Stone Age folk who lived at Skara Brae.

On the sandy shore of the Bay of Skaill on the west coast of Orkney a whale has been cast up by the sea. Men are hacking off chunks of flesh which their womenfolk pile into big whalebone basins. Children chase one another round and over the top of this mountain of flesh. Everyone is chattering, 'Here is food; here is plenty.' The cattle and the sheep are left unguarded on the pastures. The seabirds are not being hunted to-day and the shore is not being combed for limpets.

An old man sits on a stone to rest.

'The sea has been good to us,' he murmurs. 'Now no one need starve. There is food here for many moons. Look at these huge bones. Why, we can make new supports for our roofs.' He points towards a jumble of connected domes where smoke rises. 'We can make more basins to hold water and milk. We can have plenty of borers and scrapers. Our women will be pleased to have new awls to sew together our clothes of skin. They can boil the blubber and get plenty of oil for cooking. This big skin would make clothes for all of us, but we shall use it to re-roof our houses to keep the rain out. Yes, the sea has been kind.' He picks up his knife of split beach-pebble and returns to help the excited, toiling men.

When they are tired from their labours, they carry the flesh, the blubber, the bones, and the skin towards the rising smoke. They seem to be walking into the side of a hill. Do they live in the ground? No, they have constructed their dwellings at Skara Brae very cunningly. On the ground they have carefully placed flat slabs of stone, and on these piled more stones on top of one another in the shape of a square, with the walls sloping slightly inward. As the winds from the sea can penetrate walls built without mortar and make the houses cold and draughty, the people pile their rubbish outside the walls until the spaces between the eight huts are completely filled in. They may be living in their own midden but they do keep the heat in and the strong winds out.

To enter their huts they have to keep their heads down. Inside, they dump their loads of flesh beside the hearth in the middle of the room, where the peat fire is burning low. The mother sets to work attending to the fire, filling up her cooking pot and setting it to boil. Soon they are sitting on their beds, eating their supper of stew. It all seems strange to us, but this is their home and now they are happy in it. Their single room is roughly six or seven paces across. (You can compare this with the size of your classroom or a room at home.) Whalebones form the rafters for the roof of whaleskin, and there is a hole in the roof by which the smoke finds its way out.

All the furniture is made of stone, because no trees grow on the islands. At each side of the fire, at floor level, is a bed like a box of stone with a canopy of skins over it. In these box-beds the people sleep on heather and dried grass, covering themselves with skins. At one end of the room stands a dresser made of stone, holding pots and basins on its shelves. There, and in recesses in the walls, the people keep their belongings.

Besides having tools like scrapers and borers, they made themselves beads from bones and from the ivory tusks of the walrus. In the smaller bed in the house at Skara Brea, almost certainly the woman's, were found beads, and also pots with colour in them, which shows that they decorated themselves—no recent custom this! Animal bones found in the beds tell us that the family chewed the meat from them there.

Theirs were peaceful lives and they had no weapons of war. It was no human enemy that turned out the folk of Skara Brae, but the encroaching sea and sand. They left in a hurry, leaving everything as it was, even the beads from a necklace which snapped as someone scurried along the passageway to safety.

The settlement of Skara Brae disappeared under a blanket of sand. Now archaeologists, 'digging for history', have been able to reveal a clear picture of life in Orkney so many years ago.

Farming

If a hunter is unsuccessful he has nothing to eat. The New Stone Age settlers from Europe, however, had learned to domesticate, or tame, animals, and they brought cattle and sheep with them. The list on page 9 shows you that sheep were not native to this country. People now hunted less, for their herds of cattle and sheep made their supply of milk and meat more reliable. It was difficult to keep animals during the cold winter months. Many were killed in autumn. The others were fed on hay, twigs, and leaves, seaweed, whalemeat, and bark, chopped up and boiled in water. Meat was hung up to dry in the wind to help to cure it.

Stone axes and tools of flint made attacks on the forest easier. Men used to fear the forests, which were dark and full of wild animals, but gradually they conquered them and made of the trees useful friends. Wood was valuable for building huts and boats. Often the trees were felled and burned to encourage fresh grass to grow for feeding the herds and to provide new land for growing grain. Men

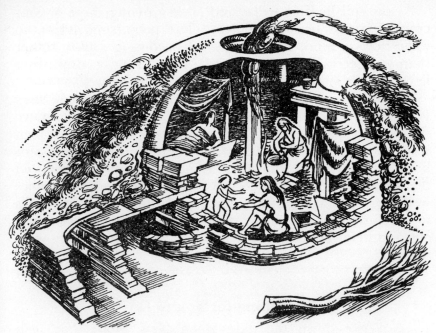

A Skara Brae Dwelling

either scattered their seeds and raked them among the wood ash, or they made holes with a stick, put in barley seeds and covered them with soil. They made sickles for harvesting by using pitch to fix sharp flints into a wooden handle, and they cut the barley stalks not far below the heads. The best seeds from the year's harvest were kept for sowing the next year.

You may wonder how we know that these people grew barley. Several jars known to have been made in the New Stone Age have marks of barley seeds on them. The seeds must have become embedded in the clay when it was still wet.

The women spent about an hour every day grinding the corn into flour by working a rubbing stone backwards and forwards on a big smooth stone called a quern. After mixing the flour with water or milk, they baked bread or cakes on stones warmed by the heat of the fire.

As the soil became exhausted after growing three or four crops, harvests became poorer. The people moved on to clear new ground, but they were becoming *settlers* rather than wanderers. A more abundant food supply meant that fewer people starved and the population increased.

We should not think that the New Stone Age people were very poor and uncivilised. Certainly their needs were simple, but they must have had enough food to feed men who had specialised jobs, like stone masons. The magnificent burial mound of Maeshowe in Orkney, for example, required the labour of many skilled craftsmen. They handled stones weighing as much as three tons, and built dry-stone walls so carefully that the edges of the stones fitted exactly into one another. Here some great chieftain and his family were buried.

Something for You to Do

1. (a) Write down the date when New Stone Age men began to land in Scotland.
   (b) Beneath it, write this year's date.
   (c) How many years ago did the New Stone Age men come?
2. Try to find out more about the achievements of the early civilisations in Egypt and Mesopotamia.
3. (a) Make a list of the tools and weapons made from flint.
   (b) Opposite each one, write down what it would be used for.
4. What do you consider were the three greatest discoveries made in the New Stone Age?
5. (a) Why did the people of Skara Brae use stone furniture?
   (b) Why did they leave their homes?
6. (a) Note the things at Skara Brae which most surprise you, and show what they were used for.
   (b) Draw a plan of the inside of a Skara Brae house.
7. Add to your chart on food, shelter, and clothing what you have learned about people in the New Stone Age.

Chapter 3

MEN WHO USED BRONZE AND IRON

Left to their own resources, the New Stone Age farmers would have had to wait many centuries before someone discovered metals. While they were working with stone tools, the people of the lands round the Mediterranean Sea had learned to mine and smelt copper. In ancient Egypt copper implements were used for two thousand years. Then, about 2000 B.C., someone in Europe discovered that when a small quantity of tin was added to copper and heated, bronze, a harder metal, was formed. The *Bronze Age* in Europe had begun. We still use bronze at the present day. Look in your pockets and see if you have any 'coppers'. Pennies and halfpennies are made of bronze.

If you look again at the Time Chart at the beginning of this book, you will notice that the Bronze Age lasted for about sixteen hundred years, about the same time as all our history since the Romans left Britain, and that metal came into use gradually and never completely. In the Bronze Age, stone axes continued to be used and men still tipped their arrows with flint. The people at Skara Brae, as we have read, knew nothing of bronze, although they were living on Orkney at the time of the Bronze Age in Scotland.

As the population increased and farmers moved from one area to another to start new settlements, struggles to decide who was to hold a piece of land must have become more common. As a result, weapons which had been made originally for hunting came to be used in war.

It was from Ireland that the knowledge of metals came. Having ample supplies of copper and gold, and being in closer touch with Western Europe than the inhabitants of Scotland, the people of Ireland soon became highly skilled in the working of metals. The smiths there made weapons and tools of bronze which they carried across the sea to trade like tinkers with the people in Scotland. Because of trade and the arrival of Irish smiths who settled in Scotland, people were able to use bronze not long after its discovery in Europe.

Near the southern tip of the mainland of Shetland, in the village of Jarlshof, people lived in oval houses solidly built of stone. When he entered, the stranger found himself in a central room where a peat fire burned. On each side he could see into the little round cubicles—the other rooms— which had walls and roofs of stone. The largest room at the far end housed the cattle. As the inhabitants were living so close to one another, they were probably members of the same family.

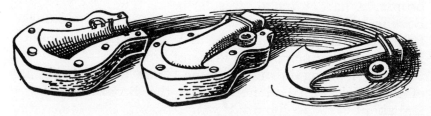

BRONZE AXE-HEADS AND MOULD

In a cell near the entrance a bronze-smith set up his smithy, and used clay moulds to cast axes and swords. The weapons were exactly like those made by the smiths in Ireland. He must have set off from Ireland or the Western Isles, and settled down to work at his trade among the people of Jarlshof. Few craftsmen can have worked under greater handicaps, for tin had to be imported from Cornwall and charcoal for the furnace from the mainland, except when enough driftwood was cast up on the shore.

The Bronze Age house at Muirkirk in Ayrshire was a stone circle measuring thirty-five feet across. The wall was low and thick. In the centre, the trunk of an oak tree held up the roof. The people and their animals lived in the same building.

BRONZE AGE HOUSES AT JARLSHOF

When the women were not cooking or grinding corn they turned their hands to making their own pottery and cloth. Using clay, they produced many of the things they needed in the home: ladles, spinning whorls, pots and bowls for cooking and keeping food. They shaped the clay with their hands and cooked it in an oven until it was hard.

They made cloth from wool. After being plucked and combed, the wool was spun, that is, twisted to give it strength. A woman held the raw wool wrapped on a stick called a distaff. She pulled a length of wool and attached it to a stick which had a whorl as a weight on the end. This she held in her other hand, and by twisting the stick spun the yarn. Then the yarn was woven into cloth on a simple loom.

In some places blue-petalled flax was grown and harvested by hand to be made into linen. Dyes from local plants and berries allowed the cloth to be coloured. For the first time people were wearing clothes not made of skin.

SPINNING AND WEAVING

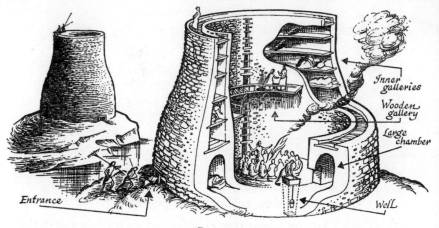

BROCHS

The Coming of the Iron Age Celts (about 200 B.C.)

The Celts arrived in Britain armed with iron weapons. Some came north overland while others left the north of England by sea and landed on the banks of the Tweed, Forth, and Tay.

They were fierce conquerors, organised in tribes. Their warriors loved fighting and kept a record of the number of men they killed. The ornaments they wore, the decorated trappings on their horses, and the quality of their weapons marked them out as proud fighters, jealous of their reputation in war. Led by their chiefs, they rode in chariots, which were as formidable in battle then as the tank to-day. Their priests, the Druids, were revered as guardians of the law, poets, and advisers to the chiefs. The Celts conquered the bronze-users, whom they forced to work for them.

Many of the farmers lived in undefended farmsteads, but the unsettled times forced some of them to build wooden palisades to protect themselves. Others sought shelter in villages behind high stone ramparts. Their settlements became not simply homes to live in but also forts for defence.

Four different types of settlement grew up in Scotland:

1. Brochs
2. Gallic forts
3. Hilltop villages
4. Crannogs.

1. Brochs

The *brochs* of the north were the biggest and most imposing buildings erected there before the Middle Ages. They were great round towers with massive walls of unmortared stones. The entrance, a low tunnel, could be blocked by a barred door. The central courtyard, with a well and an open fireplace, was the scene of day-to-day life and work. It was partly covered over, above head-level, by a wooden gallery, two or three storeys high, held up by wooden posts. A spiral staircase led up to the places where people slept and kept their belongings. Inside the broch, people were safe from their enemies. The sheer, solid walls could not be climbed on the outside, and they were too thick to be shattered by a battering-ram.

The broch men sometimes built near the coast, and always on good farming land. They had learned that a field left fallow and used as pasture for animals would soon recover its strength and produce good crops.

2. Gallic Forts

Between Inverness and the Tay, forts were built on hilltops and defended by walls of stone constructed on a framework of wood. In the fort at Finavon in Angus the rampart was over twelve feet high and twice as wide, stretching for 300 yards round the hilltop. Inside the walls were round wooden huts on foundations of stone and turf. In Gaul (France) such forts were named *Gallic forts* by Julius Caesar.

A GALLIC FORT

A Hilltop Village

3. Hilltop Villages

In the south-east the people lived in villages on hilltops, or at least above the arable land. Traprain Law, an important tribal capital, was a hilltop town covering an area of thirty-two acres. The walls of the round houses were made of wattle and daub, that is, they had a framework of interlaced sticks plastered with clay or mud. The folk there lived by farming and manufactures. Oxen were trained to pull the plough, and were prodded with iron-tipped goads. The first evidence of a plough has been found at Blackburn Mill in Berwickshire. Wool was plucked, spun, and woven to make clothes. Glass armlets, bronze dress fasteners, pins, brooches, and mountings for harness were all made by craftsmen in the town. These ornaments, and also wool and cloth, were traded with other tribes.

4. Crannogs

Just as some of the Celts sought safety on hilltops, others, especially in Ayrshire and Galloway, used surrounding water to protect them from wild animals and human enemies. In some lochs, natural islands were inhabited. More often the islands were man-made, and on each a hut or cluster of huts was erected. These are called *crannogs* or lake dwellings.

Great wooden uprights were driven into the bed of the loch to give the artificial island its main support. The uprights were connected by flat beams of oak, through which they fitted like mortised joints. Within this framework layers of stones, branches of trees, tree trunks, and brushwood were placed to raise the island safely above the level of the water. On this foundation wooden huts were built. In Dowalton Loch in Wigtownshire there were several crannogs. At Milton Loch, west of Dumfries, the house was round, walled with logs, and thatched with rushes. On the platform round the house the men dried their nets. The fire was inside the house on a hearth of flat stones.

How did the people reach their island homes and prevent their enemies from doing so? Usually they made canoes from hollowed-out tree trunks about twenty feet long and two feet deep. Sometimes they made a zig-zagging road under the water, by which a native could wade to and from the shore. Sometimes, as at Milton Loch, there was a paved causeway.

Iron began to replace bronze, not because it made better weapons but because it was easier to produce and therefore cheaper. It was used widely for farm implements like ploughs, hoes, and sickles. Land was cultivated more easily and more of the forest was cleared for farming.

A CRANNOG

Other materials were still used: bone for combs, for needles, and for the dice used for playing a game; stone for pot lids, spinning whorls, querns, and lamps; and bronze for jewellery.

You will notice that Scotland was not united. Many different families and tribes occupied it, building different kinds of homes and making a living by keeping herds and growing crops. Their chariots, showing their knowledge of the wheel, their pottery, and their ornaments, demonstrate that they were not uncivilised, although they were less civilised than the next invaders, the Romans.

Something for You to Do

1. Give the answers to these questions about bronze:
   (a) Which two metals are used to make it?
   (b) Why does bronze make better weapons than copper?
   (c) How did bronze tools come to Scotland?
   (d) Under what difficulties did the bronze-smith of Jarlshof work?
2. Draw a Bronze Age house.
3. Write a paragraph describing the Celts preparing for battle.
4. (a) On a small map of Scotland show where the four different kinds of Iron Age dwelling were.
   (b) Draw the kind of settlement that was common in your district.
5. Under the heading of 'Traprain Law' make a list of the things made and used there which show that the people were civilised.
6. Write notes on: brochs; Gallic forts; wattle and daub huts; crannogs.
7. Add to your chart on food, shelter, and clothing what you have learned about the people of (a) the Bronze Age and (b) the Iron Age.
8. The book *Warrior Scarlet* by Rosemary Sutcliffe will tell you more about life in the Bronze Age.

Chapter 4

THE ROMANS COME AND CONQUER

The last of the Mediterranean civilisations was that of Rome. Having subdued the Latin farmers of central Italy, the Romans gained control of the whole country. Carthage, a trading city across the sea in North Africa, challenged the Roman power, and her soldiers under Hannibal crossed the Alps and advanced almost to the gates of Rome. But the Romans rallied, and wiped out the city of Carthage. During the two centuries before Christ, the Roman legions marched and fought and extended their power over all the lands round the Mediterranean—'The Sea in the Middle of the Land'.

Julius Caesar

To their previous conquests, the great general Julius Caesar added Gaul (France), from which he sighted this land, which he called *Britannia*—'The Land of the Britons'. His two invasions, in 55 and 54 B.C., which brought Britain into recorded history, were unsuccessful, and served only to show to the Britons the existence and power of Rome.

Not long afterwards, Rome became an Empire, under Caesar's nephew Augustus, and it was during his supremacy over Judea that Jesus was born. Nowadays, when we wish to give the date of an event, we say that it took place a certain number of years *before* or *after* the birth of Christ. The letters 'B.C.' beside a date, stand for the words 'Before Christ'. The letters 'A.D.' mean 'After Christ'. They really stand for two Latin words—*Anno Domini*—which mean 'In the Year of our Lord'. So, when we say '50 B.C.', we mean ' fifty years *before* Christ was born', and when we say 'A.D. 50', we mean 'fifty years *after* Christ was born'.

The Roman Conquest of Britain

The serious conquest of Britain began in the first century
A.D., when the Emperor Claudius despatched legions to
these shores. The south and east of the country were taken
only with difficulty, and, while the Romans were trying to
conquer the tribes of north Wales, Boadicea, the queen of
the tribe of Iceni in the east, led her people in revolt and
recaptured London, burning the town and killing thousands
of Romans. The revolt was crushed, and the Romans
pushed on westwards and northwards.

Agricola

The task of making Britain into a Roman province was
entrusted to a new governor, Julius Agricola. He was both
a wise ruler and a skilful general.

Once the people in the north of Wales had been subdued,
southern Britain became settled. At each of the Roman
fortresses, York, Chester, and Caerleon-on-Usk, a legion of
crack troops was stationed, and long, straight roads were
built to allow them to move quickly to any trouble-spot.
Legionaries from York, for example, could march north
along Dere Street to deal with raids by the Caledonians.
South and east of a line between these three fortresses,
Britain prospered under Roman rule.

Where there were soldiers, there was money, and where
money, trade. Garrison towns attracted traders, and new
towns grew up at river crossings and at places, such as Lincoln,
where roads crossed. The Roman farm was called a *villa*,
and was a large range of buildings with barracks for
the labourers. British landowners copied these villas, and
increased their output of food so much that they were able
to feed the townsfolk and the Roman soldiers. New vegetables
such as the cabbage, the beetroot, and the pea were introduced, and fruit trees such as the cherry. British tribal
chiefs began to wear the toga, and their sons learned to
write Latin. They paid taxes to the Romans, and benefited
from the *Pax Romana*, or 'Roman Peace'.

The Romans in Scotland

About A.D. 80, Roman legions crossed the Cheviots into *Caledonia*, as they called Scotland, and Agricola built a line of temporary forts between the firths of Forth and Clyde. North of the Tay, he established a great fort at Inchtuthil, fifteen miles from Perth, which was capable of housing an

entire legion of 5000 men. From this base he tried to conquer the North. Some of the native forts are now called *vitrified forts* because their timber-framed stone walls have been burned with such intense heat that the material 'ran together'. The burning used to be blamed on the Romans but probably the natives did it themselves to form solid defensive walls.

The Celts saw nothing of Roman civilisation, only the damage done by the Roman soldiers. 'They make a wilderness and they call it peace,' said Calgacus, a Celtic chief.

In A.D. 84, Agricola fell on the northern tribes at the battle of *Mons Graupius*. Many of the Celts were killed, and the rest driven into the hills. Before Agricola could continue

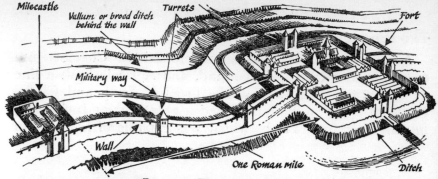

PART OF HADRIAN'S WALL

his invasion of the Highlands he was recalled to Rome, but he had made Scotland, south of the Forth and Clyde, part of the Roman Empire.

Under pressure from the raiding Celts from the north, the Romans were later forced to withdraw from Scotland altogether. A line between the Solway Firth and the Tyne was chosen by the Emperor Hadrian for building a wall, which became the northern limit of the Roman Empire.

Hadrian's Wall

As it remains to-day, this wall is by far the largest and most spectacular historical ruin in Britain. It stretches more than seventy miles from sea to sea. In front of it is a deep ditch, and behind it runs a straight road connecting the forts. Built by the Roman soldiers between A.D. 122 and 128, the wall is eight feet wide, faced with dressed stones on either side, and filled in with rubble between the stone blocks. It is thought to have been fifteen feet high.

Along the wall were a series of strong forts, on the same pattern as Newstead[1] but smaller in size, each being able to house from 500 to 1000 men. Between them, for every mile of the way, were milecastles, where guards looked out constantly over the bleak moorland for signs of marauding Celts. The soldiers who manned the wall were auxiliaries recruited from tribes all over the Empire: among them were Belgians, Germans, and Spaniards.

[1] See next chapter.

Antonine's Wall

In A.D. 142, the Romans occupied the south of Scotland again, and, as Agricola had done earlier, chose the line between the Clyde and the Forth as the new frontier. Here they built a new boundary of turf and clay on a stone foundation. It was shorter than Hadrian's Wall, running for thirty-seven miles from sea to sea. In front was a ditch, twelve feet deep and forty feet wide. Twenty feet behind it they raised up a huge mound of turf, fifteen feet wide at the base, ten feet high, and six feet wide at the top. The soldiers did all this work. One inscription reads: 'In honour of the Emperor . . . Antoninus Augustus Pius, father of his country, the Second Legion, Augustus's own, completed [the work of the wall] for 4652 paces'.

At intervals along the wall were nineteen forts, roughly one every two miles, and behind it a military road was constructed, with a surface of gravel on top of big stones lying on a bed of clay. The soldiers in the forts were guarding the northern limit of the might of Rome.

Something for You to Do

1. Write notes on: Hannibal, Julius Caesar, Boadicea, Agricola.
2. Which three towns in Roman Britain had legions stationed in them?
3. In what ways did the people in the south of Britain benefit from the presence of the Romans?
4. Make a map of Roman Scotland, showing Hadrian's Wall, Antonine's Wall, Newstead, Inchtuthil, Cramond, Inveresk, and the Roman roads.
5. If you cut through Antonine's Wall, you can look at it *in section*. From the measurements given on this page, and using a scale of one inch to ten feet, draw a *section* of the ditch and wall. Show the direction of North.

Chapter 5

THE ROMAN SOLDIERS
AT NEWSTEAD

A Roman Legionary

Agricola made a wise choice
in building the Newstead fort
on a ridge commanding the
crossing of the River Tweed.
Situated roughly half-way between the Tyne and the Forth,
Newstead became the main centre for controlling the south-
east of Scotland. The fort was square with rounded corners,
the shape of all Roman forts. It was defended by two ditches,
and by a massive rampart and stone wall which enclosed an
area of fifteen and a half acres.

Within the defences, the buildings were laid out as the
diagram shows. In the centre was the main building, which
was used as the headquarters of the fort. The standards and
pay-chests were kept there. On one side of it was the commandant's house, and on the other the officers' quarters.
The commandant's house was centrally heated by a hypo-
caust, a fire from which hot air passed under the floors and
through pipes in the walls. Nearby stood the granaries,
with their floors raised above ground level to keep the grain
dry. To the east were the barracks of the legionaries, the
Roman infantry. The legionaries were Roman citizens.
Citizenship gave them the right to marry, or hold property,
or become officials helping to control the Empire. To the
west were the buildings housing the horses and men of the
auxiliary cavalry. These auxiliaries, like the men who
defended the walls, fought for Rome but were not yet Roman
citizens.

It was obvious from the size and strength of the Roman walls and forts that the Roman soldier spent far more of his time in building than he did in fighting. He had to be prepared to do anything—to help to raise a rampart, dig drains, build barracks of stone or of wattle and daub, make roads, store grain, and cook. In addition, when Newstead was continuously lived in, the soldiers cleared the forest, cultivated the soil, and grew crops. We know this from the tools such as hoes, rakes, sickles, and scythes, which they left behind. Some of them had special jobs: some worked with leather, making and repairing jerkins, harness, boots, and shoes; some made armour from fine brass scales, laced together with leather and wire; some made weapons; and some were carpenters. Though all these occupations took up much time, the men were soldiers first and foremost, and would practise fighting for the days when they marched against the Celts or took their turns in guarding Antonine's Wall.

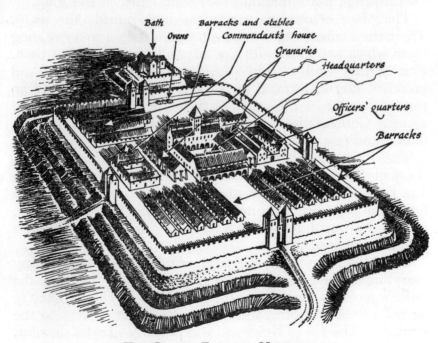

THE ROMAN FORT AT NEWSTEAD

B

Remains found at Newstead give us a good picture of the Roman soldier. He wore an iron helmet, coming low at the back to protect his neck like a German 'tin hat', and tying under his chin. His jerkin was of leather, and was covered with iron breastplates curved to the shape of his body, or with scale armour. The legionary wore breeches which reached half-way down the calf of his leg, and over them he had a skirt which looked like a kilt. His boots were heavy, with five or six layers of leather on the soles, which were tacketed.

The legionary carried a short stabbing sword with a blade twenty inches long, while the auxiliary had a long, slashing sword. Shields were normally oval, and made of wood covered with leather and bound with bronze. A short bow was used by the auxiliaries to fire arrows, which, for the first time in this country, had iron heads with three barbs. Spears too were carried. Often they were quite short ones for throwing, but sometimes they were fourteen feet long.

The place of recreation was the bath outside the walls. There the soldiers took a warm bath, moved on to a sweating room which was filled with hot air, and then into a hot bath. Finally they had a cold plunge to cool off. They did exercises afterwards, and were massaged by attendants who rubbed ointments into their skin. There too they played games. Gaming pieces, such as draughts and dice, have been found, and one soldier left a brooch behind.

The Romans occupied Newstead for two long periods, the first lasting until the Celts attacked some time before A.D. 122. Seeing the invaders sweeping into the fort in force, the Romans, outnumbered and their forces dispersed, prepared to withdraw. What would they do with their valuable equipment?

'Hide it in the wells, quickly! And in the pits! Dump everything, these bowls, that helmet, these querns, the smith's tools! Cover them up, quickly! Quickly! They're on us!' Broken swords and a cleft skull bear witness to the struggle. The loss of Newstead was part of a greater disaster, in which the ill-fated Ninth Legion was wiped out.

When the Romans returned, in A.D. 142, they rebuilt the fort, but did not find the treasures hidden by their old comrades more than twenty years before. Roman troops were stationed there for the next sixty years, longer probably than the lifetime of the average man in the second century A.D. The men who in recent years dug up Newstead fort found a sacred altar, jugs, beads, and coins among the skeletons of unburied animals and men. The Romans had suddenly been forced to seek shelter on the south side of Hadrian's Wall.

Their stay in the south of Scotland did not, as in southern Britain, result in the spread of Roman civilisation. It was a military conquest, achieved and maintained by force. A final attempt to conquer Scotland failed, and the land fell back into the hands of the Celts, although the Romans controlled the south of Britain for two more centuries. Their roads alone remained, and were used by traders for hundreds of years afterwards. Even to-day, the roads from Carlisle to Glasgow, and from Jedburgh to Dalkeith, follow the routes chosen by the Romans for many miles.

Something for You to Do

1. A football pitch has an area of about one and a half acres. Newstead fort covered fifteen and a half acres. How many football pitches could have been contained within its walls?
2. Find out what the following words mean: auxiliary, infantry, cavalry, rampart.
3. Study the tools found at Newstead, and write notes on their use.
4. Imagine that you are a Roman soldier in Newstead. Describe a day in your life.
5. Draw a Roman soldier with his weapons.
6. An exciting book on the Romans in Scotland is *Word to Caesar*, by Geoffrey Trease.

Chapter 6

THE MAKING OF SCOTLAND

A period of four hundred years, as long as that which separates us from John Knox and Mary Queen of Scots, is a remarkable time for any Empire to last, especially when it is controlled from a single city. Neither Rome nor Italy could recruit enough troops to man the defences. More and more of the conquered peoples were enrolling in the Roman armies, until not even the generals were of Roman birth. The Roman Empire had become too big, its army of civil servants too burdensome. Great men struggled for power, while the poor struggled to keep their families and pay their taxes. The Empire did not, however, collapse because of revolution within its borders, but because it could not withstand a new threat from outside.

The Barbarians

It is difficult at first glance to see how Britain could be affected by happenings in eastern Asia. At that time, however, the grasslands there began to dry up, and this set the people, the Huns, on the move. Prevented from swooping on China by the Great Wall, which had been erected in defence against them, these fierce, yellow-skinned, and black-haired men turned their shaggy ponies towards the setting sun and swept all before them. The movement of the peoples was on! Fearless horsemen, firing bone-tipped arrows as they rode, they crossed the Urals and the Steppes of Russia. Unable to withstand these cruel conquerors, some of the Germanic tribes, called Goths, sought safety within the Roman Empire. They were the people who formed new kingdoms in the west, West Goths in Spain, East Goths in Italy, Franks in France.

The Romans tried to face the new danger by giving up their more distant conquests and concentrating their forces nearer home. But the capital was captured by Alaric the Goth in A.D. 410, and the greatness of Rome was at an end.

The Making of England

Britain was now undefended and open to attack. The peoples of the lower Rhine valley—the Angles, Saxons, and Jutes—were caught up in this movement westwards.

Leaving their villages, the separate tribes of Angles, Saxons, and Jutes gathered their weapons and rowed across the North Sea in open boats. Keen seamen, they thought a shipwreck was a good way of gaining experience.

They swarmed round the river mouths, penetrating as far inland as possible before landing. If you look at a map, you will notice that most rivers in Britain flow towards the east, making invasion from Europe easier. On landing, the invaders fought the Britons, driving them slowly westwards into the highlands of Cornwall, Devon, Wales, and the Lake District. The Roman forts and towns they looted and destroyed. Not used to town life, the

Anglo-Saxons settled on the banks of rivers or cleared the forests to build villages and cultivate fields as they had done in Germany. Gradually the kingdoms of *Northumbria* (north of the Humber), *Mercia*, and *Wessex* (occupied by the West Saxons) were formed, and by the tenth century were united into *Angle-land* or 'England'. The newcomers brought their own language, English.

In Wales to-day, many people still speak their own language, Welsh, which is derived from the common speech of the ancient Britons. It may surprise you to learn that the same language was spoken in Scotland also, by the Britons of Strathclyde.

Four Peoples in Scotland

The movement of the peoples affected Scotland too. North of the Forth, the people became known as the Picts or 'painted men', from their habit of painting their bodies. We know nothing of their language, but we do know that they were fierce heathens, who had been a constant menace to the Roman province. They have left ample proof that they were artists in stone, who carved figures of animals, horsemen, and footsoldiers on flat slabs. They covered by far the largest area of the country, but much of it was mountainous and unproductive land, and the people were widely scattered. In the south-west were the Britons, whose capital was at Dumbarton.

So far, we have used the word 'Scotland' to describe our native country, but have made no mention of the Scots. We have, in fact, been describing Scotland before the Scots. Two new peoples arrived—Angles from the east, sailing up the Forth and Tweed, and Scots from the west. The Angles drove the native Britons westwards into Galloway and the Clyde valley. The Scots came in skin-covered boats from Ireland to form their kingdom of *Dalriada* in Argyll. This small, sea-girt kingdom of Gaelic-speaking Scots, though cut off from the rest of the country by mountains, was, in time, to give its name to the whole people.

How did these four peoples become united? There can be no doubt that the spread of the Gospel by the followers of Ninian and Columba gave the people something in common to outweigh the divisions by mountain and language. At that time, it was not certain that Scotland as we know it would ever become an independent kingdom. The Angles of Northumbria controlled most of the land from the Humber to the Forth, and swept northwards into Pictland. In A.D. 685, however, 'God favoured Brude mac Bile', and under him the Pictish warriors overwhelmed the Angles at *Nectansmere* near Forfar. This great victory made sure that the land, north of the Tay at least, would remain independent.

In A.D. 843, Kenneth MacAlpin, King of Scots, became king of the Picts as well. He seems to have had a claim to the Pictish throne through his mother, at a time when the Scots were receiving reinforcements from Ireland while the Picts were suffering from Viking raids. This explains why the Scots triumphed and the country came to be called 'Scotland' and not 'Pictland'.

The people between the Forth and the Cheviots were included in the northern kingdom by the middle of the eleventh century. The Angles of Lothian in the east were certainly under the rule of King Malcolm II of Scotland by 1018, after his victory over the English at *Carham-on-Tweed*. Sixteen years later, Malcolm was succeeded as king by his grandson, Duncan, king of the Britons of Strathclyde. With the exception of the lands in the north and west in the grip of the Vikings, the whole of Scotland was now subject to one king.

Something for You to Do

1. What were the reasons for the fall of the Roman Empire?
2. Name three kingdoms formed by the Goths in Europe.
3. Name the early kingdoms formed by Anglo-Saxons in England.
4. Draw a map to show the four peoples who made up Scotland.

5. (a) Which people occupied your part of the country?
   (b) Try to find out something about their settlements, chiefs, saints, etc.

   You will find clues in the names of places, like those in the chart below, for example.

Name	Language	Meaning	Place
Pit	Pictish	Bit of farmland or farm steading	*Pittodrie* (croft by the wood, or, on the slope)
Bal	Gaelic	Village	*Ballindalloch* (village in the field) *Bellahouston* (village with the crucifix)
Caer	British	Fort	*Caerlaverock* (fort of the lark) *Cardonald* (fort of Donald)
Ton	English	Village	*Symington* (Simon Lockhart's toun)
Ham	English	Home	*Oldhamstocks* (old homestead)
Field	English	Field	*Ashfield* (field with the ash trees)
Ford	English	Ford	*Deskford* (ford over the dark stream)

6. Make a time-chart, covering the years from A.D. 400 to 1100, and insert the main events from this chapter. Keep adding to it as you read on.

Chapter 7

THE COMING OF CHRISTIANITY

He died that we might be forgiven,
He died to make us good.

You have probably met or listened to a missionary home from India or Africa, and heard him describe how he lived among the natives, teaching the children, healing the sick, and telling about the life, the example, and the death on the Cross of Jesus Christ. In the early centuries after the birth of Christ, our ancestors had not heard the Gospel— the 'good news'. *They* were the heathen peoples, and to them the missionaries came.

We know little about the religion of our ancestors in early times. The people were mystified by the world around them, and worshipped what they welcomed but did not understand. Led by the Druids, they worshipped the rising sun, the giver of light and warmth. Beltane feasts and Hallowe'en are modern reminders of early religions.

St. Ninian

Ninian grew up among the Britons, and went to Rome to be educated. There he was eventually made a bishop, and joined the great St. Martin at Tours. St. Martin taught him to go away on his own to think and pray, and then to return to the world to spread the word of God. He became our first missionary, when he returned to live among the Britons, in the 'no man's land between Roman and Pict'. In A.D. 397, he and his helpers built the first church in Scotland, at *Whithorn*. They covered its walls with white plaster, and it was known as the 'white house'. This was the headquarters of the mission, where they prayed and

DECORATION FROM THE 'BOOK OF KELLS'

worked and ate together. There local chiefs sent their sons to school and young missionaries were trained, and from there the missionaries set out, dressed in cloaks of undyed wool and carrying book and staff, to brave the weather and the suspicions of the folk in the hill-top forts. They converted the people of the south-west, and, working north and north-east, built churches at Glasgow, Eccles near Stirling, Dunottar, Methlick in Aberdeenshire, and as far away as Navidale in Sutherland.

Many places have a connection with a local saint. Glasgow, for example, claims St. Kentigern (Mungo), Culross in Fife has St. Serf, whose retreat ('desert') was, tradition tells us, at Dysart. Can you find out who was the missionary in your district? Often the oldest church, the parish church, is dedicated to St. Mary, but the names of other churches sometimes provide clues to local saints.

St. Columba

The Scots, as you will remember, came to Argyll from Ireland. It was from Christian Ireland that Columba came, not as a young man dedicated to the Church, but as a high-born prince disgraced in his own country. A quarrel over the ownership of a copy of the Psalms which he was making led to a battle which drove him to exile himself. In A.D. 563, he set out to find a place from which he would not be able to see the shores of Ireland again.

He and his twelve companions pushed off in their boats in the direction taken by their fellow-Scots in Dalriada. Tossed like corks on the Atlantic waves, they came at last to the windswept island of *Iona*, off the west coast of Mull. Here was a place of loneliness and silence, yet near enough to the Scots of Dalriada, and here they built their church. They were a simple, self-supporting community, living in separate huts round the church, with only such other buildings as were necessary. There was the kitchen, the guest-house (for they made a 'fuss' of strangers), the stable, the workshop, and the granary. They kept flocks, ploughed the land, and fished. Like the followers of St. Ninian they lived humbly, having nothing to call their own. Columba himself had only a stone for a pillow.

They loved learning. Had not Columba's departure from Ireland been due to the secret copy he had made of the Psalms? Lovingly they copied the sacred words of the Gospels, and an example of their work, which was begun in Iona, is the beautiful *Book of Kells*, now in Trinity College, Dublin. Learning to write was tiring and difficult, because the standard of decoration was so high, as you can see from the illustration.

> My hand is weary with writing,
> My sharp quill is not steady
> My slender-beaked pen pours forth
> A black draught of shining dark-blue ink.

They paddled their little boats to the northern islands, such as the Isle of Skye. They penetrated the long sea lochs, and travelled across Perthshire and Fife, bringing to the Picts the story of Christ. Columba himself, fearless of robber and wolf, reached Inverness, where he converted Brude, King of the Picts.

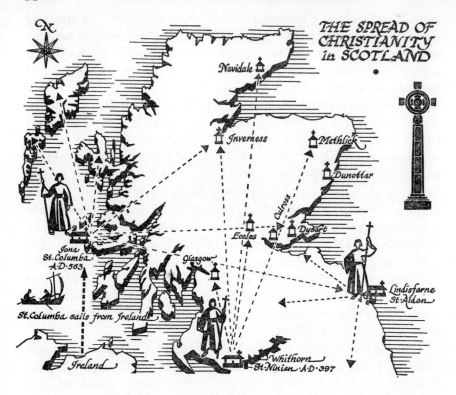

For years Columba watched over the work of his disciples, making Iona the religious centre of the north. He was a strong, rugged, commanding figure, but at the same time a kind, friendly man, who loved children and animals. When he was very old, and knew that he was going to die, he climbed the slope above the church and blessed the island with these words:

> Unto this place, small and mean though it be, great homage shall yet be paid, not only by the kings and peoples of the Scots, but by the rulers of barbarous and distant nations with their people. Thy saints also, of other churches, shall regard it with no common reverence.

So indeed they have, and with reason. Christianity, shared by Pict and Scot, led them to join together as one nation. St. Aidan left Iona and made *Lindisfarne* (Holy Island) his home for the task of converting Northumbria (which included what is now south-east Scotland). To continue Aidan's work, St. Cuthbert left his sheep on the Lammermuirs, to tend a human flock.

Most of England, however, received the Gospel from St. Augustine and his followers, who were sent from Rome. The adoption of Roman Christianity in southern England, and eventually, by the decision taken at the *Synod of Whitby* in A.D. 664, in Northumbria as well, helped to unify the English, and to separate them from the northern peoples, the children of Whithorn and Iona.

St. Andrew

'Why', you may ask, 'is St. Andrew the patron saint of Scotland?' This is the reason. Andrew, the first of Jesus's disciples, was crucified on a *saltire*, or X-shaped cross, in Greece. Some of his bones were carried to a church in what is now the town of St. Andrews in Fife, and this church became the most important in Scotland. St. Andrew's Day, the 30th November, is remembered, particularly by Scots abroad, as Scotland's special day, and his cross has become the national flag.

Something for You to Do

1. Make a drawing of Columba's settlement in Iona, as you imagine it looked.
2. On a map of Scotland mark the places visited by the followers of (a) St. Ninian, and (b) St. Columba.
3. Who converted the district where you live? Think about the names of churches, halls, stations, and streets which are called after saints.
4. Under the heading 'Iona', copy into your notebook the blessing of St. Columba on the island.
5. Draw St. Andrew's Cross (white on a blue background).
6. A good book about Columba's time is *The Eaglet and the Angry Dove*, by Jane Oliver. If you want to learn more about St. Andrew, you should read R. K. Hannay's book, *St. Andrew of Scotland*.

Chapter 8

THE VIKINGS

It is high tide on Iona, on a summer morning in the year 806.

The shepherd looks out to sea, attracted by the screeching of sea birds. There's a boat with a sail, another and another, eight in all, riding proudly on the waves. He peers into the distance in fear. Can it be . . . ? He sees the raven on the sail of the foremost ship. The Vikings are coming, the demons, the plunderers, the killers. He runs through the heather, down the slope to the church.

'They're coming, they're coming!' he screams. The brothers understand at once. There have been raids before.

The bell tolls. The abbot comforts the monks and leads them in prayer. He orders the ornaments and precious writings to be hidden, and walks out to meet the invaders. They are landing now from their long, narrow boats, which they have cast up high on the sand. Look at them—tall men, fierce men, with round shields, terrifying battle-axes and swords. The abbot stands before them, pleading with them to leave his church in peace. They brush him aside, and rush to the settlement. Some make for the byre, drive

46

the cows down to the shore, and kill them there. They need the meat for food. Most of them hurry into the church. They catch the monks storing their treasures under stone slabs. Axes swing, swords flash, and monks fall dead. With straw and a light the church is set on fire. The brethren outside kneel and pray, but are put to the sword. Sixty-eight people on the island become martyrs, and the Vikings go back to their ships, laden with treasures and supplies.

Who were these invaders? How and why did they come?

The Vikings

They were great sea warriors, who came from Scandinavia. If you look at a map of this land, made up of Norway, Sweden, and Denmark, you will see that much of it is mountainous, and that the west coast is cut into by a great many *fiords*. In the time of the Vikings the hill-land was poor, so that the men looked to the sea for a living. Having discovered how to make iron, they made tools to cut down trees, and used the wood to make boats. They fished, but soon the sea beckoned them further, and they became explorers and raiders.

They built two kinds of boat. One of these was quite small, narrow, and shallow in draught, and was used for summer raids. The other was wider and deeper, with the head and tail of a dragon, and was driven by oar and sail on long sea voyages.

On their early expeditions, the Vikings sailed in their smaller ships to plunder other lands. Naturally, the best places to raid, in their eyes, were those in which the booty included not only food, drink, and clothing, but also gold and silver ornaments to take back to their womenfolk. This is why holy places suffered so many attacks, and why the monks feared the Vikings and welcomed the bad weather, as an Irish monk tells us in the margin of his manuscript:

> The bitter wind is high to-night;
> It lifts the white locks of the sea.
> In such wild winter storm no fright
> Of savage Viking troubles me.

The Vikings returned home to spend the winter building boats, making weapons, eating, drinking, and telling stories in their halls high above the fiords. Their love of adventure, their urge to outdo their rivals, and their feeling for the sea made them great sailors and explorers. With no instruments (they knew nothing of the compass, for example), they sailed in their great ships to new lands—the Shetlands, the Orkneys, the Faeroes, Iceland, and Greenland. Usually they sailed westwards, reaching out towards the setting sun. They found their way by using rough-and-ready rules. Sailing to Greenland, for example, they passed the Faeroes at a distance from which the sea appeared halfway up the mountains. They sailed south of Iceland at a distance from which wild-fowl and whales could be seen, and westwards to a point in Greenland just north of Cape Farewell. Can you follow this voyage of the Vikings on a map?

The Vikings as Settlers

Erik the Red discovered Greenland and settled there. His son, Leif Erikson, was the first man to sail direct from Greenland to Norway and back. Later, about A.D. 1000, while searching for timber to make boats, Leif Erikson sailed along the coast of North America, which he called Vinland. This was nearly five hundred years before Columbus 'discovered' America.

For centuries the Vikings searched for lands which were like their own but better than their own, where they could live in the same way but make a living with less effort. They became land-winners or settlers in the lands which they explored. Under the leadership of Ruric, they entered and gave a name to Russia; under Rollo they occupied Normandy, the land of the Northmen in France; under Guthrum, and later Sweyn and Canute, they settled in England. Shetland, Orkney, Caithness, and Sutherland, the Hebrides, Ireland, the Faeroes, Iceland, and Greenland became Viking lands, and the North Atlantic, as it were, a Viking lake.

The Viking *Sagas* tell of hardships met with, and heroic deeds performed, while these new lands were being found and

conquered.   They tell us who the foremost Vikings were.
Some warriors were given surnames according to their looks
—Harold Fairhair, Erik the Red, Helgi the Lean, and
Onund Woodenleg; some according to their dress—Ragnar
Hairy-breeks and Magnus Bareleg; and some according to
their reputation in battle—Erik Bloodaxe and Thorfinn
Skullsplitter.

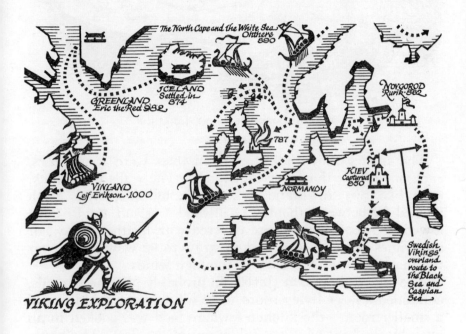

VIKING EXPLORATION

They were not merely destroyers.   They kept their links
with the sea by pirate raids and slave-trading, but they
fished as well, and even used boats for moving crops of hay.
They settled in lonely parts of Scotland like Jarlshof in
Shetland.

The position of Jarlshof was as attractive to the Vikings
as to Stone Age and Bronze Age peoples more than two
thousand years earlier.   The land was fertile, and cod could
be caught and grey seals hunted.   Besides, Viking ships
called there from Orkney on the way to Norway, only
forty-eight sailing hours away.

VIKING LONGHOUSES AT JARLSHOF

The homes they built for themselves were longhouses, each one longer than a cricket pitch. The walls were thick, each like two 'dry-stane dykes' side by side, with earth packed in between them. Driftwood was cut up to form low-ridged roofs which were covered with heather, straw, or sometimes peat. Stones tied to straw ropes were hung over the thatch to keep it secure in the high winds.

The oldest house at Jarlshof, probably the headman's, contained a large living room, with a fire in the middle, and a smaller room—the kitchen—where food was cooked in an oven by the heat of stones taken out of the fire. The house was smoky, and peat soot covered the rafters. The other two houses had people and animals living under the same roof. They were 'clarty but cosy'. The outbuildings included a byre, a barn, and a smithy, where a hole worn two inches deep in a stone anvil is proof of constant hard hammering by the smith, who made everything from sickles to fishing hooks. Between the buildings were paths of stone slabs, and in the yard were stone platforms on which hayricks stood.

The work of the people of Jarlshof changed with the seasons. There was sowing in the spring, followed by lambing, sheep-shearing, hay-making, harvesting barley, and slaughtering

some of the animals before winter set in. They cut peats
and dried them in the sun on the hill across the bay. They
enjoyed fishing in summer. The sheep-shearing saw the
start of another year's cloth-making. Washing, combing,
and spinning followed one after another until, during the
winter evenings, cloth was woven on an upright loom by the
light of little oil lamps. All the year round there were
the cattle, sheep, and pigs to herd, and in the winter the
cows were kept in the byre-stalls. The men killed many
calves, lambs, and young pigs for food. They caught fish
and killed sea-birds to give their meals some variety. Usually
they ate flesh and fish only, bread being kept for feasts.

These crofter-fishermen at Jarlshof were typical of thousands of Vikings who settled on the islands and the mainland
of Scotland, bringing with them their knowledge of sea-faring
and boat-building. The dialects and names of places in the
northern islands show how far their conquests spread. For
centuries they were a threat to the power of the Scottish
kings, but they did bring courage, strength, and a spirit of
adventure to Scotland. Some of us are descended from them.

Something for You to Do

1. Make a map showing the countries where the Vikings
   settled.
2. Name the islands and counties settled by the Vikings in
   Scotland.
3. Make a list of countries settled by the Vikings, the
   coasts of which have many fiords.
4. Why is one of the counties in the north of Scotland called
   Sutherland?
5. How many surnames like the Viking ones on page 49
   can you find or make up?
6. How did the Vikings who settled in Jarlshof make a
   living?
7. Draw a Viking ship.
8. If you are interested in the Vikings, you will enjoy reading
   The Land the Ravens Found, by Naomi Mitchison.

Chapter 9

MALCOLM CANMORE AND ST. MARGARET

By the time of the reign of Malcolm III (1057-93), Scotland
was a united country, covering roughly the same area as
to-day. True, the islands and north mainland were subject
to the Vikings, but elsewhere the king's word was law.
Though the people recognised Malcolm Canmore [1] as
king, it is doubtful if they yet thought of themselves as the
Scottish nation. Local chiefs still had great power. Nor
did all the people speak the same language. Pictish was
dying out, and Gaelic was becoming the language of the
Highland folk. In the south of Scotland, English was
spoken in the east and was coming to be used in the west.
There were also differences in religion, because not all
Scotland had been converted by St. Columba.

In the north the people lived in hamlets, keeping animals
and hunting, while round the villages of the south-east
more corn was grown, because the land was more fertile
and the heavy plough had been introduced.

Malcolm Canmore

With so many races in Scotland, it is not surprising that
Malcolm's own background was mixed. Half Celtic, half
English, he 'had the Gaelic' and spoke English as well.
His father, Duncan, had been killed by Macbeth, who then
seized the throne, and Malcolm had had to seek refuge in
England. During his years in England, he had come to
know something of how it, and the other countries in Europe,
were ruled. Here too, although Malcolm was never able
to read or write, he had met and admired men of learning.
Finally, he had returned to Scotland and defeated Macbeth

[1] *Canmore* was Malcolm's Gaelic nickname. It meant 'Great Head'.

at the battle of *Lumphanan* in Aberdeenshire. He was now king of Scotland, and set up his capital at Dunfermline.

The Norman Conquest of England

While Malcolm was king in Scotland, England was successfully invaded from Europe. The Normans, who were descendants of the Vikings, came to England from Normandy in France, led by their duke, William. They had become Christian and French-speaking, and had lived under the most efficient government in Europe. Training and practice made them skilled fighters on horseback. They defeated the English at the battle of *Hastings* in 1066, and William became king of England. The story of the invasion is shown in pictures in a magnificent piece of needlework called the *Bayeux Tapestry*, which was made not long afterwards.

Harold, the king of the English, had been killed at Hastings. Edgar, the Saxon heir to the throne, had to flee with his family from the Norman conquerors. They came north by sea, and landed on the south coast of Fife, in a bay between Rosyth and North Queensferry, which is now known as St. Margaret's Hope. The refugees were made welcome at Dunfermline, where Margaret, Edgar's sister, became Malcolm's queen.

St. Margaret

Margaret must have seemed to the Scots a woman of strong will and expensive tastes. She delighted in the 'show' of royalty. When the king travelled, he was now escorted by a strong bodyguard of retainers on horseback. The royal palace became a blaze of coloured fabrics; the royal table was decked with gold and silver dishes and goblets. Margaret's demands encouraged trade, especially in luxuries.

It should not be thought that Malcolm had married a queen who dominated him and imposed her own foreign will on Scotland. He had found a partner who shared his own desire to make Scotland a more modern, more religious, and better governed country. Together they could take the best of what they knew of Europe as their model. **Certainly** she helped him to rule the country, the only woman to take part in controlling Scotland till the time of Mary Queen of Scots.

Had she not married, Margaret would have entered a convent and become a nun. An intensely sincere and religious woman, she did all she could to help the poor. Her ladies learned that she disapproved of riotous laughter. They copied her gracious manners, and followed her example in doing good.

Margaret used her influence to encourage religion in Scotland, bringing the country more into line with the ways of Rome. Monks were invited to Dunfermline, and began to build the great abbey there. Pilgrims were housed on either side of the Forth, and were ferried across free of charge on their way to St. Andrews.

On hearing the news of Malcolm's death, during an attack on the north of England, Margaret died in Edinburgh Castle, where her small chapel still stands. Her tomb beside that of her husband in Dunfermline Abbey became a place of pilgrimage, for Margaret was remembered as a saint.

St. Margaret's Chapel, Edinburgh Castle

Something for You to Do

1. In Malcolm Canmore's reign, how did people make a living, (a) in the north, (b) in the south-east?
2. Copy a scene from the Bayeux Tapestry.
3. What did Margaret do, (a) for the king, (b) for the Church?

A NORMAN KNIGHT CHARGING AT HASTINGS
From the Bayeux Tapestry

Chapter 10

DAVID I AND NORMAN WAYS

Although William had been crowned king of England, he still had to campaign against the English until he had gained control of the whole country. He had also to reward his followers. This he did, not with money, but by settling them on newly-conquered land. Norman lords were given areas of land on condition that they swore to obey the king, and brought a fixed number of knights to fight for him when required. In this way, a lord became the king's tenant or *vassal*, holding land in return for military service. Lords who held land directly from the king were called *tenants-in-chief*. They did not normally wish to keep a large number of knights in their own houses. Instead, they retained a large area of land for themselves, and gave the rest to their tenants. These *sub-tenants*, as they were called, swore an *oath of homage* to become 'the lord's man', and undertook to provide a certain number of knights. Sub-tenants in turn might sub-divide their lands, keeping part for themselves, and dividing up the rest among various knights who became their vassals. This system of land-holding is called *feudalism*.

How did the Normans differ from the English? They were foreigners who spoke French, gained land, and became a new landed aristocracy. They were *over* the English. Roughly speaking, they were the lords and knights, and the English became serfs and had to work for them. They were knights, trained to fight on horseback. For protection they wore a *hauberk*, a long leather coat covered by metal rings, with a slit in front to allow them to sit comfortably on horseback. The helmet was cone-shaped, with a strip of metal coming down in front to protect the nose. The lance was their chief weapon. They occupied castles at important places, to make sure that the English did not rise against them. They even looked different, with their shaved chins and their hair cut short at the back and sides.

David, Earl of Huntingdon

To avoid the turmoil in Scotland after the deaths of Malcolm and Margaret, their younger children were sent to England to be brought up. David was received at the court of William Rufus, where he became a scholar and a knight. This enforced holiday is important in our history because England was the channel through which many of the latest European ideas reached Scotland, and it was David who brought them.

David was, by rank, Earl of Huntingdon, besides possessing many other lands in England. He was one of the chief nobles at the court, while his high character and wisdom made the new English king, Henry I, respect his advice. David saw English government at work from the inside. He served an apprenticeship second to none.

David and the Normans

The Normans came to England as invaders and remained as conquerors. Scotland suffered no Norman conquest. The Normans came north by invitation. When David became King of Scots, he brought some of his Norman friends with him. Many of their names are familiar to us to-day—names like Bruce, Corbet, Riddell, Lindsay, Montgomery, Graham, and Somerville. Normans who followed later included Melvilles, Fairbairns, Balliols, Archibalds, and Oliphants.

Feudalism in Scotland

In Scotland, as in England, feudalism was introduced. The newcomers were given land, on condition that they brought knights to fight for David. For example, De Brus (Bruce) was given Annandale in return for the service of a hundred knights. He swore an oath of homage to the king, promising 'to be his man', and of *fealty*, like this:

> I, Robert, swear on these holy Gospels of God that henceforth I shall be faithful to you, as a vassal ought to be to his lord. You will never lose life or limb, nor the honour you have, by my will, advice, or encouragement, but in all those things I shall be your helper according to my power.

This arrangement served the king well. In return for the land they held, the lords promised to obey him. Notice that they did not own the land, for it was all the king's: they 'held' it. Even to-day, by the law of 'treasure trove' in Scotland, anything found on or in the ground belongs to the Crown. 'What belongs to no one belongs to the king.' Each lord governed his region for the king, enforced the king's laws, and collected his taxes. From the king's point of view, it was the most satisfactory way of ruling the country, and it provided him, whenever he needed it, with an army of cavalry which cost him nothing.

The king would go to the lands he granted and pace out or ride the limits, pointing out boundary marks like 'the old oak tree', or 'the big round stone', since there were no maps. Details of the lands granted and services due were recorded on a *charter*, which was signed and sealed before witnesses. This was the lord's legal title to his land. It was also the first evidence of written government, the work of an early civil service of churchmen, chosen because they were the only people who could write.

The land of a lord or sub-tenant, became known as his *domain*. Near its centre was his tower or fortified house. Close by arose the church, and in this way the country became divided into parishes corresponding in size to the lord's domain. The priest had the protection of the lord, and his help in the collection of *tithes*, the tenth of every man's produce from the land, which was due to the Church to maintain the priest and the poor. The finest existing Norman parish church in Scotland is at Dalmeny, near Edinburgh. Notice in this picture the rounded arches over its door and windows:

THE PARISH CHURCH, DALMENY

Royal castles were built throughout the land. Wherever there was a royal castle David would station a Norman baron as sheriff, to maintain law and order in the surrounding countryside. This area usually developed into a *shire*, with the castle, and later the town which grew up beside it, as

DUNDRENNAN ABBEY: Founded by David I

its centre or capital. The sheriff was also in charge of defence and the collecting of taxes, although to-day his main duty is to deal with more serious offences brought before his court.

Sheriffs, and indeed all tenants-in-chief, could expect periodic visits from the king and his court. The government was not fixed in one place but mobile, accompanying the king on his travels throughout the land. In this way the king could find out for himself what was going on in all parts of his kingdom. Besides, his lords owed him hospitality, and he could keep himself and all his retinue by living for three or four days on the feasts provided by each one.

Burghs, Abbeys, and Trade

The royal castles were signs of the king's power. The abbeys, founded by the monks whom David had invited from England and France, showed his efforts to make Scotland more religious and more civilised. When he made certain villages into royal burghs, he took the first important step to encourage industry and trade. The first Scottish coins—silver pennies—were minted at Roxburgh and Berwick during his reign. Previously, foreign coins had been used. Though the use of money was not yet common, trade with foreign countries was made easier. Measurements too were laid down. An inch was the length of three good barley grains laid end to end, while an *ell*, roughly a yard, measured thirty-seven inches.

In all these ways, David I made Scotland a more advanced country, and gave it a pattern of life which was to last for four hundred years.

SILVER PENNIES
From the Reign of David I

Something for You to Do

1. Why was feudalism useful to the king in Norman times?
2. In class, choose a king, one tenant-in-chief, sub-tenants, and knights. Now act the ceremony of swearing an oath of fealty. Each man swears the oath to the lord immediately above him, and, if that lord is not the king, he should add the words, 'except the faith that I owe to the king'.
3. Has anyone in your class a Norman surname? If so, write it down, with as many others as you can think of.
4. Make a list of all the ways in which Scotland became more modern in the reign of David I.
5. In some churches you can see monuments showing knights, and in some churchyards there are carvings of weapons on grave slabs. Corstorphine Church in Edinburgh has some interesting monuments. Can you find any others?

Chapter 11

SCOTLAND IN THE MIDDLE AGES

1. *Life in the Castle*

The first castles in Scotland were all royal castles. When the king was going to build a castle, he had to ask himself,(1) *Is a good water-supply available in case of siege?* (If you visit Edinburgh Castle, look for the two wells.) (2) *Is the position easy to defend?* Usually, an outstanding crag or hillock was suitable, preferably at a loop in a river, or where two rivers met. Where no hillock was available, one might be made. A ditch was dug in a circle, and most of the earth thrown inwards to make a huge mound. The ditch, whether it was filled with water or not, was called a *moat*, while the mound was called the *mote*. This is probably the explanation of the mote at Hawick, which formed a man-made base for a wooden castle.

> Upon a great dark-coloured rock
> He had his house right nobly set
> Built all about with wattle-work
> Upon the summit was a tower
> That was not made of stone and lime.

None of the early wooden castles has survived to the present day, but the stone-built Duffus Castle near Elgin is built on the early pattern. If you were a friend approaching a castle, you would cross the bridge over a deep and wide ditch filled with water from the nearby stream. A sentry would open the strong door, the only entrance, for the castle was surrounded by a vast wall of earth crowned by a wooden palisade. You are now in a flat, grassy area, called the *bailey*. On the right of the track you see the byres and stables and enclosures into which all the beasts will be driven

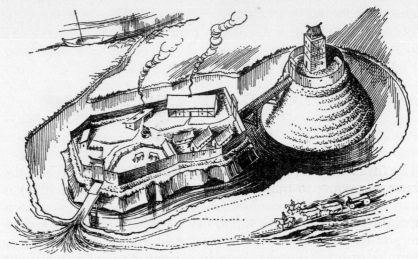

A MOTE AND BAILEY CASTLE

tonight for safety. On the left, servants are carrying a side of
beef to the kitchen, which is attached to the hall. There,
by the big fire, you will eat and be entertained, in the company
of everyone except the sentries.

You dismount, a man leads off your horse to the stable,
while you cross the bridge to the *mote* and clamber up the
steps to the tower. You pause and look up. The tower is
plain and solid, built of hefty timbers, but plastered with
clay to lessen the risk of fire. Here you will meet the baron
and his family, who live and sleep in the tower. The sentry
on duty on the battlements looks down, recognises you, and
waves his hand. You are now in a *mote and bailey castle*.

Stone Castles

Wooden mote and bailey castles were the main strongholds
of the kingdom for close on 200 years, but the cramped
accommodation in the tower, and the danger of destruction
by fire, drove men to start building with stone. Stone castles
were generally more spacious, and differed considerably in
shape from one another, according to the type of site on

which they were built. Caerlaverock in Dumfriesshire, for example, which was built on an island in a marsh, was triangular in shape, with great round towers at two corners, and a formidable gateway flanked by two towers at the third. Rothesay Castle, by contrast, is circular, while Kildrummy in Aberdeenshire is rectangular, opening out towards its gateway.

Stone castles, which are built as places to be safe in, have thick walls, some as much as nine feet in width. The two main buildings are the tower and the hall. As the weakest part of the castle is the doorway, the occupants do all in their power to strengthen it. A drawbridge may prevent enemies from reaching it. An iron-grilled portcullis is dropped down in front of the iron-studded door. The top of the tower is reached by a dark spiral staircase, rising and turning clockwise to deny a right-handed attacker freedom to slash with his sword. The sentry patrols the platform walk on top of the battlements, looking out for friend or stranger moving towards the stronghold.

As we have seen, all the early castles belonged to the king. During the fourteenth and fifteenth centuries, however, when kings were weaker, the barons erected castles for themselves. They built with stone, insisting on very thick walls to stand up to attacks from cannon. The walls were strengthened until they were fourteen feet thick in places. Into the building of Borthwick Castle near Edinburgh went 30,000 tons of stone.

In time, even the smaller landowners—the lairds—built towers as fortified dwelling-places. These towers, or their ruins, can be seen all over Scotland to-day. Usually built in the shape of a rectangle, some have a wing attached, making an L-shape to provide more rooms and more comfort. Inside the tower, the layout of rooms was similar to that in the castle.

The hall became the centre of castle life as kings and barons demanded higher standards of comfort. We know, for instance, that James II did not 'rough it' in Edinburgh Castle, for he was provided with a feather mattress and a

pillow, wine, and salmon. The king's room at Stirling had
glass windows. The palace at Falkland had a park and
gardens laid out for the king to enjoy. For exercise he could
play tennis, while indoors he could have a game of cards or
chess, or play his guitar. What he did the barons copied.

In spite of these improvements, it is doubtful whether we
should have considered a castle comfortable. Gay tapestries
covered some of the stone walls and a rug lay by the fireplace,
but most rooms were entered through arches without doors,
and the wind whistled through the long, narrow window-
slits, which had to be stuffed with rags in winter. The castle
was draughty and dark. At night, fir splinters or lamps
burning fish or animal oil gave some light but made the
rooms smoky and smelly. Floors strewn with rushes became
refuse heaps of scraps from the tables. Dogs wandered
about. The place smelled of food and filth, animals and
people. Though washing hands at the table was an established practice, people seldom washed their entire bodies.
One writer has in fact described the Middle Ages in Europe
as 'a thousand years without a bath'. All the rubbish and

CAERLAVEROCK CASTLE, DUMFRIES
In Medieval Times

IN A CASTLE HALL

slops from the castle were tossed into the moat. Better not to be thrown in there yourself!

The hall was the place where the lord ate in company and in public. He, his family, and his guests, sat at a raised table, served by squires. The 'salt-fat' or large container stood in the centre of the table, and poorer people had to sit 'below the salt' or else at separate tables. The food was placed on the table, and the important people helped themselves first. Dishes were of silver or wood, and a dagger was useful for cutting meat. For eating, people used spoons and their fingers, as forks had not yet been invented. When the meal was over, people stayed in the hall and drank, told stories, listened to the minstrel, or laughed at the jester. The ladies span and wove, made elaborate tapestries, and sewed napkins and cloths.

The men in the castle were concerned with its defence and its supply of food. Large stocks of food were kept. Many animals were killed in November, then cured and hung in the cellars, while the granaries were kept full of grain. Pepper and other expensive spices were bought from merchants to make their food more tasty. A baron

C

had always to be ready to feed the king and his retainers, for this was part of his duty. Hunting in the forest, which was wasteland rather than woodland, was an enjoyable pastime and a source of fresh meat.

Attached to the larger royal castles, you would meet men of many different occupations—*bailies* who collected taxes, *fletchers* who made arrows, *lorimers* who made spurs and stirrups, porters (door-keepers), as well as tailors and cooks, foresters and falconers. Many of them were busily at work in the outbuildings in the bailey. John the cook and William the falconer became known as John Cook and William Falconer, and here we have a clue to many familiar surnames.

Something for You to Do

1. Make a drawing of a mote and bailey castle.
2. Go and see the castle nearest to your home. Make a drawing of it, showing the different rooms, stairs, etc. Find out:
   (*a*) Who built it.
   (*b*) Why it was built there.
   (*c*) Where the stone came from.
3. Make a list of these technical terms and their meanings: *mote, palisade, bailey, hall, drawbridge, portcullis, moat, fletcher, lorimer.*
4. (*a*) *Boys*: Write an eye-witness account of 'How we defended the castle against an enemy attack'.
   (*b*) *Girls*: Write about 'My day in the castle'.
5. Make a model of a mote and bailey castle. A shoe-box will serve for the tower. Fit match-boxes together to make turrets at the corners. Battlements can be cut from cardboard and stuck on to the top. The surrounding wall may be made by joining match-boxes together. The whole tower and wall should be painted the colour of wood or stone.
6. This sentence will help you to remember the difference between a *mote* and a *moat*:

   'You could sail a b-o-a-t on a m-o-a-t'.

Chapter 12

SCOTLAND IN THE MIDDLE AGES

2. *From Serf to Freeman*

In modern times, we think of the 'country' as being away from the towns and cities where most people live. We talk of going out 'into the country', among planted woodlands and isolated farms large and small. But in Norman times nearly everybody lived in the country, not on farms standing on their own, but in hamlets or little groups of houses called *touns*. 'Ton' at the end of the name of a place, such as Symington or Haddington, means a 'toun' or village, and tells us where many of them were and who founded them.

There were a few towns, not of great importance at first, and these were called *burghs*. They were really touns which had been promoted to positions of more importance by kings or barons or the Church.

The Toun

When David I granted land to Norman barons or to the abbeys, the touns and the people in them were all fitted into the scheme of feudalism. Every piece of land had its lord, and in David I's reign a law said that if there was any man 'that hes no propir lord', he must find one within fifteen days or be fined eight cows. Every village became subject to a lord or to an abbot, if it were on land granted to monasteries, and the men had to perform certain duties for their lord in return for the lands they held. Some were free but most were serfs. Some were sold, such as Turkil Hog and his sons and daughters, who cost the Prior of Coldingham three merks of silver. Halden and his brother William and their family, on the other hand, were given by the Earl of

67

A Toun

Dunbar to the Abbey of Kelso. Serfs belonged to their masters, and wore iron collars which showed what they were and whose men they were. They could not leave the toun or change their jobs. Thus they were not free, but they had some land, and in those unruly days it was often better to have a lord's protection.

The lands of the toun were worked as a whole, the men helping one another to perform the tasks in the fields. They had to provide everything they needed within the village. They farmed to feed and clothe themselves, and this is called *subsistence farming*.

Not all land was cultivated. Marshy tracts along the river bank were avoided. The rest of the land was divided into two parts—the patches of *infield,* nearer to the toun, which were constantly under cultivation, and the *outfield,* rougher, more distant, and probably higher, which was used for pasture. From time to time, some parts of the outfield were ploughed and cropped but not manured, until the yield was so low that they were allowed once more to lapse into pasture. To grow crops year after year on the same soil, manure is needed, and manure from the byres and wood-ash from the cottage fires were carted out to the infield. This arable land was divided into long strips called *rigs* or ridges, ploughed up and down the slope to let the water run off. Each villager held scattered strips to ensure that good and bad land was equally shared, and the system was called *run-rig.*

The heavy wooden plough had from eight to twelve oxen yoked to it to pull it. Since none of the villagers owned so many oxen, each contributed one or two to make up the plough-team. At least three men were required to handle the plough. One man guided it from behind, another put his weight on it to keep the blade in the furrow, while the third man controlled the oxen. Turning them was difficult, because they were yoked together in pairs and not harnessed like horses. This probably explains why the strips were long and narrow. They allowed as much land as possible

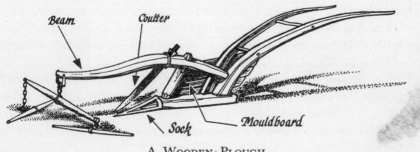

A WOODEN PLOUGH

to be ploughed with the least number of turns. Other workers would be busily removing big stones and breaking up stubborn clods of earth with wooden mallets. Seed was sown broadcast by hand, and weeding was an endless task.

When harvest-time came, mowers stooped to cut the corn with sickles. Binding and stooking were done by hand. Oats was the main food crop, for it made oatmeal and oatcakes, while barley was grown for brewing into beer. Peas and beans, cabbages and kale were the main vegetables; turnips and potatoes had not yet been introduced to Britain.

The cattle and sheep of the village grazed on the outfield under the eye of the 'toun-herd', who was ever on the look-out for wolves. About November, when food for the animals became scarce, the most weakly ones were slaughtered. The beef and mutton were salted to provide a stock of food for the family throughout the winter.

In the Highlands and other hill areas, less of the land was cultivated and herding was more common. On high land which was difficult to reach or where only small patches of ground could be tilled, the spade and the *caschrom* took the place of the plough. Using the latter, twelve men could turn over an acre in a day. The caschrom has been called an early plough, but in using it a man works backwards and turns the soil from right to left, that is, in the opposite way to the plough.

Besides growing crops and keeping animals, the people had many other tasks. There was wood to collect and peats to cut, flax to cultivate and linen to spin and weave, sheep to shear and cloth to make (usually the 'hodden grey'—undyed wool), all jobs in which boys and girls could help.

The old dwelling-house might have to be repaired or rebuilt. It was probably built of stone on a wooden framework and roofed with turf or heather. The usual hole in the roof, which was not directly over the fire, was all there was as a chimney. Inside, all was dark, when the wicker door and the window-shutters—used instead of glass—were closed. As in the houses of the Vikings, the cows were often under the same roof.

Roof of heather and rushes

Bed of straw

Wickerwork door

A MEDIEVAL COTTAGE

Furniture was home-made—a table, a bench to sit on, combs, spindles, whorls, and a loom for making cloth. The family slept in holes in the wall, or on straw or heather on the earthen floor. Since there was little housework to be done, women spent most of their time making cloth and helping in the fields.

At Medilham (Midlem) toun,
on the land of the Abbey of Kelso, in 1250.

It is just after sunrise on a September morning, and a husbandman and his son are milking their cows.

'It will be a fine morning to start the harvest,' says the father. 'We should manage to cut one rig of oats to-day, with your mother and the girls to help. Go and sharpen the sickles when you finish with that cow.'

'Yes, father,' replies Adam, 'It will be a change from weeding. The weeds grow as fast as we can cut them.'

But as he goes out of the byre, he hears a voice, the voice of a man on a shaggy pony, the steward from the Abbey grange—

'Come on, all you men! All of you to the grange to cut the corn for the Abbey.'

'But we are going to cut our own corn,' mutters Adam.

'Quiet, boy,' his father reproves him—'We must do as we are told.'

'We shall need you all till the crop is cut,' the steward goes on. 'You husbandmen must do five days' work, and the cottars must come till the work is finished. Come to-day, and every dry day until you have done the service you owe.'

'Reaping and carrying their corn, shearing their sheep, ploughing their land,' thinks Adam, fingering his iron collar. 'I wish we had only our own work to do.'

By 1290, Adam had his wish. The husbandmen of Medilham had each twenty-six acres of land, at a rent of eleven shillings a year. They had a struggle to pay the rent, for eleven shillings was a lot of money in the Middle Ages, but at least they were now free men.

And, by the time the Scottish nation had won its independence at Bannockburn in 1314, many more Scottish people were free tenants of the land they farmed.

Something for You to Do

1. Find from a map as many touns as you can in your district. Remember that 'ton' in the name of a place means a toun.
2. Under the heading *Subsistence Farming*, make two columns, the first giving the crops and animals of the toun, and the second saying what they were used for.
3. Usually a plough-team could plough an area of 220 yards by 22 yards in a day. Find out how many square yards there are in this area. Does this figure mean anything to you?
4. Learn the names of the parts of a plough.
5. What were the advantages and disadvantages of being a free man?
6. Make a drawing of a toun.
7. Make a model of a peasant's house. Use plasticine for the walls, which should be roughened to look like stone. Tie twigs together in pairs to form the rafters, and stick the ends into the tops of the front and back walls. String between the twigs will hold the roof of hay or foam rubber. String weighted with stones at each end may be laid over the thatch to hold it down.

Chapter 13

SCOTLAND IN THE MIDDLE AGES

3. *The Rise of the Burghs*

'*The Royal and Ancient Burgh of* . . . .' Many a burgh in Scotland is proud of being royal and more ancient than its neighbour. This reminds us that burghs did not simply grow out of small villages. A burgh was *created* by being given a charter, a grant, written and sealed, of its rights, privileges, and duties.

If a burgh gained its charter from the king, it became a *royal burgh*, if from a lord or from the Church a *burgh of barony*. The distinction became important in later times, because royal burghs sent representatives to the Convention of Royal Burghs, and to Parliament. In David I's reign, there were fourteen royal burghs—Aberdeen, Berwick, Crail, Dunfermline, Edinburgh, Elgin, Haddington, Inverkeithing, Linlithgow, Perth, Renfrew, Roxburgh, Rutherglen, and Stirling. Most of these, you will notice, have given their names to shires. Lying in the shadow of a royal castle, they were centres of the king's government, and became county towns.

William the Lion was another king who founded many burghs. Examples of burghs of barony created by lords are Prestwick and Kirkintilloch, while Glasgow, St. Andrews, and Canongate—which was then separate from the royal burgh of Edinburgh—are of the same type but created by bishops or abbots.

Though a charter was a sign of a burgh's foundation, it could not guarantee its prosperity. Burghs were, above all, places where people traded, and they rose and decayed according to their geographical situations. Ports like

73

Aberdeen, Dunbar, and Irvine flourished on fishing, and Dumfries and Berwick on the rich lands beyond them, the latter exporting most of the wool from the Border abbeys. Stirling grew up where an important route crossed the Forth.

Trades and Trade

The burghs were a new stage in the story of how men made a living. The townspeople did not have to meet all their needs by doing everything for themselves. They learned a trade and specialised in it, making things to sell, such as shoes, or doing a service for which people were willing to pay, like shoeing horses. The money they earned gave them freedom of choice—they could buy what they wanted. Merchants lived completely by trading, that is, by buying goods and selling them at a profit. Towns near castles benefited from the presence of people with money and expensive tastes. There was a ready sale for wines from France, fine woollen cloth from Flanders, honey, onions, figs, and spices such as pepper, cinnamon, and nutmeg.

The People in the Burghs

Some families had always lived in the burgh. But if serfs escaped from their lords, and held a toft or piece of land in the burgh and were free for a year and a day, they too became burgesses. Men from England or Normandy who were skilled in some craft might be admitted, and merchants from Flanders, known as *Flemings*, came to settle. Later, however, when crafts became organised, members of each trade used their influence to keep newcomers out. In

A Rich Merchant

the larger towns, especially in the ports, the merchants formed a merchant *gild* or company, which often gained full control of burgh affairs.

Town Councils and Freedom

At first, burgesses paid rents for their separate tofts to the king's officials, the provost and bailies, but many burghs saw that they stood to gain by running their own affairs. An annual sum of money, paid to the king by the burgh as a whole, secured independence. In 1319, £213. 6s. 8d. was paid to the king by the town of Aberdeen. In this way the burgesses became free men and, equally important, the provost and bailies and 'good men of the better, more discreet and more trustworthy of the burgh', chosen by the burgesses, formed the town council. Thus the burghs became self-governing communities of free burgesses.

What a Burgh Looked Like

By our standards, the burghs were extremely small, more like present-day villages in size. The townsfolk still relied on the land for much of their food. Their cows were collected and driven out to the common by the town-herd early in the morning, and brought back for milking in the late afternoon.

We watch the merchants' servants and other townsfolk weeding the town's land—'the burgh acres', as it is called—on our way to the East Port. This is one of the gates in the wall around the town. Soon we reach a wider area, the market place, and there in the middle is the Mercat Cross. This is where the weekly markets are held, proclamations read, taxes paid, and dues collected from strangers trading in the town. Nearby is the little parish church. The market place narrows at one end into the Hie Gate or High Street, often the only street. Notice the cobble stones, sloping downwards to a drain in the middle of the street to let the water run away. Piles of filth clutter the street, the place smells. Small wonder that plagues are common!

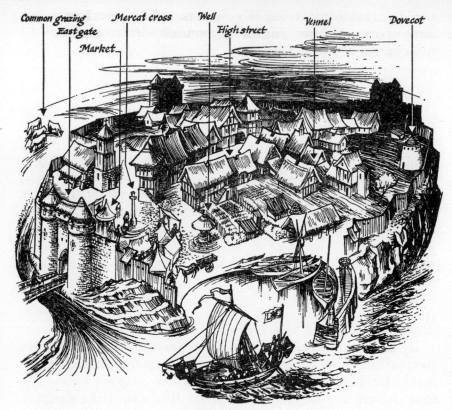

Common grazing   Mercat cross   Well
East gate   High street   Vennel   Dovecot
Market

AN EARLY BURGH

The little houses, built of wood and with thatched roofs, face the street. Everyone likes to live in the High Street, and, where a piece of land has been split, we find two narrow houses with their gable ends to the street. Behind the houses there used to be gardens stretching as far back as the burgh wall, but now, with more people coming to live in the town, building land is scarce. Closes or *vennels* branch off at right angles to the High Street. The burgh has developed in the pattern of a fish-bone, with the High Street as the main bone.

Enclosing the burgh is a wall of stone or earth with a palisade on top, which the burgesses maintain. They keep **weapons** in their houses to take with them when it is their turn to keep guard after the gates have been closed for the night. This happens at curfew time, when the bell tolls to warn the townsfolk to damp down their fires. They are always afraid of fire.

Crafts

Crafts or trades of all kinds developed. There were many smiths—blacksmiths, goldsmiths, silversmiths, and tinsmiths, Some men were skilled *websters* or weavers, *baxters* or bakers, fleshers, skinners, and glovers. Others were fletchers, lorimers, saddlers, potters, masons, and tailors. New jobs meant new surnames. Many of our streets and markets too take their names from trades—e.g. Potterow, Fleshmarket.

To learn the craft of making shoes, a boy became an apprentice for seven years. He worked in his master's workshop in part of the house. He was careful to obey his master and his master's wife too, for he lived in their house. Gradually he picked up the secrets of the trade and improved his skill until at the end of his apprenticeship he became a *journeyman* [1] or tradesman. To become a member of the craft, he had to make his 'masterpiece'—a fine pair of shoes. If his work satisfied the deacon of the craft, he could then set up in business for himself, as a master-craftsman. So it was in all the other trades.

Each craft had its own association. Rules were laid down by each craft, limiting the number of apprentices a master might employ, fixing wages and prices, setting standards of workmanship, and caring for the widows and orphans of members.

Markets and Fairs

There were no shops. Buying and selling took place on market days at stalls in the market place. Some burghs had special markets, often to be detected from street names—the Haymarket and the Lawnmarket (linen) in Edinburgh, and the Coal, Wood, and Horse Markets in Kelso. The right to hold a fair was limited to some royal burghs once or

[1] Meaning 'paid by the day'—from the French *journée* (day).

AT THE FAIR

twice a year. Luxuries brought by merchants from abroad made the countryfolk stand and stare. The work of making things in the town stopped: this was the time for selling. Acrobats and minstrels came to entertain in what was the highlight of the year.

To-day, many of our towns still have holidays and 'all the fun of the fair', even when the real reasons for the fair— buying and selling—have long since disappeared. There is still the Glasgow Fair, and the Lammas Fair at Inverkeithing.

Here are some of the rules from the charter granted by the king to Aberdeen:

1. I forbid any foreign merchant within the sheriffdom of Aberdeen from buying or selling anything except in my burgh of Aberdeen.

2. Foreign merchants will bring their goods to my burgh of Aberdeen and shall there sell them and pay his penny.

3. No one is to keep a tavern in any town in the sheriffdom of Aberdeen unless he is a knight of the town and residing in it.

4. No one residing outside my burgh of Aberdeen shall make or cause to be made any dyed or mixed cloth within the county of Aberdeen except my burgesses of Aberdeen who are in the gild merchant.

5. I forbid any foreigner to buy or sell hides or wool except within my burgh of Aberdeen.

Something for You to Do

Use the information in this chapter to learn all you can about your own and other towns. For example:

1. What kind of burgh do you live in or near? When did it gain its charter? Who granted it?

2. If you live in an old burgh, what were the reasons for its early importance?

3. What crafts were practised there? Do any of them survive to-day?

4. Did the town have a merchant gild? Is there a merchant company to-day?

5. Who is the provost? How many bailies are there on your town council?

6. In an old burgh, go out and draw a plan of the market place, high street, old closes and ports. Insert the old parish church and mercat cross. Try to find a map which will show the old boundaries of the town.

7. See how many names of streets you can find which refer to old trades and markets.

8. Does the town still have a fair? What happens at it now? What used to happen?

9. Make sure that you understand the following: tofts, masterpiece, curfew, 'pay his penny'.

10. Write a description of 'Dawn till Dusk in an Old Scottish Burgh'.

Chapter 14

SCOTLAND IN THE MIDDLE AGES

4. *The Monks of Melrose Abbey*

Among the monks whom David I brought to Scotland were the *Cistercians*, commonly called 'White Monks' from the cloaks they wore. They had gone back to the simple life followed by St. Benedict, a life of prayer and work.

Benedict was the son of a rich Roman noble. While at school in Rome in the fifth century A.D., he was so horrified by the wicked and lawless lives led by most of the people that he left his school and his home to live as a hermit in a

THE CHURCH AT MONTE CASSINO
Founded by St. Benedict

cave. It was a common thing for holy men to turn their backs on the world and to go and live in the wilderness alone. Benedict, however, was not left alone. Against his will, he attracted followers—men who wanted to give up their lives to the worship of God. He taught them to live together as a band of brothers, calling one another 'brother'. With their help he built a great church on the hill called Monte Cassino in Italy.

In the next five hundred years, monasteries were established all over western Europe. In Scotland, of course, people were used to the teachings of St. Columba and his followers, but they had been monks of a different kind, who lived in separate huts and wandered from place to place like missionaries, preaching to the people.

Benedict realised that men living together all the time needed rules of conduct. They had two main duties—to worship God (this took them into Church seven times a day), and to work. In addition, they took three vows:

1. *Poverty*—to give up all they possessed.
2. *Chastity*—never to marry.
3. *Obedience*—to obey without question the wishes of the abbot.

David I did most to bring bands of monks from Norman England and France to Scotland. His mother, St. Margaret, had established the abbey of Dunfermline. Many of his nobles and successors followed his example. He gave land to the monks, mainly on the lowlnads of the south and east. As time went on, more and more barons gave some of their lands to the abbeys, which became great landowners, holding some of the best land in Scotland. Later it was said of David that 'he left the Kirk ower rich and the Crown ower poor'.

Why did kings and nobles give presents of their lands in this way? The first reason—and this affected kings mainly—was that the monks were more learned and civilised and could do much for a backward country. Secondly, people in the Middle Ages were very religious, and their main concern was to make sure that when they died they went to Heaven. If they gave lands to an abbey, the monks would pray for their souls.

The earliest Cistercians to come to Scotland settled at Melrose, in an ideal position south of the River Tweed. The land was good and suitable for arable farming. There were rich meadows for their cows, while the gentle slopes provided pasture for their sheep. The forest supplied timber for building and fuel. Water diverted from the river drove their corn mill and flushed the great drain which took waste from all the buildings. From the slopes of the Eildon hills came a good water supply, later carried by pipes to the abbey buildings. Good building stone could be quarried nearby.

When their first simple church was completed, the brothers started to lay out all the other buildings necessary for the life of a large religious community.

In course of time, a splendid church was built of local stone by bands of masons who left their marks, but not their names, on the sections of work which they undertook.

Gradually the brothers became divided into two types:

1. The *monks*, who attended all the religious services, wrote, taught, healed, and supervised.
2. The *lay brothers*, who did not take full vows, and did more of the heavy work about the abbey, its kitchens, and its lands. Their living, eating, and sleeping quarters were separate from those used by the monks, and they had their own cloister as well.

If we arrive at the abbey after nine in the morning, we shall meet the monks coming from the church after service. This was their fourth service of the day, the first one having been at midnight. They walk slowly, silently, their heads bowed as they make their way along the cloister walk to the chapter house, where they stand quietly, the tiled floor under their sandalled feet, to hear a portion of the rules read to them, and to receive instructions for the day. Two brothers see that the church is ready for the next service of the day. Brother Reginald goes to make candles from wax for the altar. Brother John sets to work on his accounts, while the others disperse to work in the gardens or to study in the cloister. There they can only look inward, for behind them massive walls of stone shut off their eyes and their minds from the world outside.

In the stables, the horses are harnessed for a nobleman and his followers. There is the nobleman now with his two sons, saying farewell to the abbot after spending the night

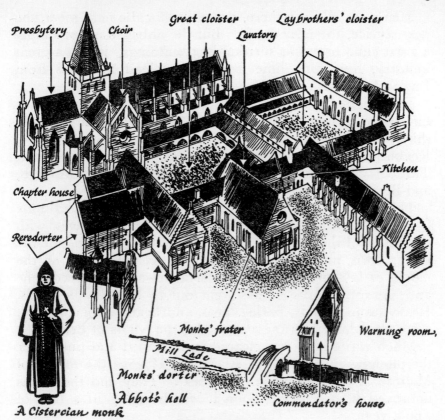

Presbytery
Choir
Great cloister
Laybrothers' cloister
Lavatory
Kitchen
Chapter house
Reredorter
Monks' frater
Warming room
Mill Lade
Monks' dorter
Abbot's hall
Commendator's house
A Cistercian monk

MELROSE ABBEY
In the Middle Ages

in his hall. As we walk towards the cloister, the voices of
the boys or novices ring out clearly as they recite their
lessons. Passing the monks' dining hall, we see the nobleman's servants loading their horses with food and baggage
for the journey northwards to spend the night at Newbattle.

As we go out through the abbey gates, the almoner is
giving bread to the poor. A heavily-laden cart, its axle
and solid wheels all turning creakingly together, trundles
along with a load of wood for the kitchen fires. And here,
wearing a cloak and a square black cap, comes a bearded
monk, an Austin canon, no doubt carrying a message
from the Abbot of Jedburgh.

Men were all busy there, preparing for the next meal, the next service, the next world. But the abbey was not simply a great church and its surrounding buildings; it was a great industry, importing lime from Kelso, lead for roofs from England, and oak from Flanders.

You might have lived many miles from Melrose and yet have been in touch with some part of its lands, in Berwickshire on the way to the sea, on the uplands of Selkirkshire, Roxburghshire, and Peeblesshire, as far west as Mauchline, Turnberry, and Maybole, or in the towns of Perth, Edinburgh, and Berwick where the monks had houses.

The monks were good farmers. The abbey had nine large farms, called granges. These were really villages, with the hovels of the serfs and their families clustering beside the byres, corn mill, and brew-houses. Usually one of the monks or lay brothers acted as farm steward. At seed time and harvest, all the monks went out to help in the fields. Heavy crops of oats, barley, peas, and beans were common, more abundant than the average for the whole of Britain.

Much waste land was cleared and drained and put under the plough. For example, Alexander II gave the monks of Melrose 'my whole waste of Ettrick'. They and their serfs improved it, and before long it was bringing in a rent of £66 a year.

Several of the monks worked in the gardens and orchards, some kept bees for their honey (there was no sugar in Scotland in the Middle Ages), and some went fishing. Many of the finest stretches of water in the Tweed and its tributaries were reserved for the monks, who must have eaten many a meal of trout and salmon.

The monks were great breeders of animals. Many oxen were required to pull the heavy wooden plough. Cows and goats were kept for their milk, some of which was made into butter and cheese. The abbey owned hundreds of horses—it is reckoned that at one time it had as many as 1400. This reminds us how important the horse was in the Middle Ages, for carrying men and goods in peace and war. The monks, then, must have been among the first horse-dealers.

They were most famous, however, for breeding sheep. The sheep, which were very small and scraggy, were kept mainly for their soft wool. They were moved up to high pastures in summer and returned to the lower slopes about September. Roads were so poor that wheeled traffic was uncommon. The fleeces were carried by pack-horses, or on sledges pulled by horses, down the slopes of the Cheviots and Lammermuirs to the abbey, and along the valley to the port of Berwick. There the monks owned land and store-houses, where the wool was stored until ships were ready to carry it over to Flanders where it was made into fine cloth.

This trade made the abbey wealthy, but it helped the king and country too, for the king received customs duties from the wool which was exported, and so the increase in trade brought much-needed money into the country.

When you visit an old abbey, try to imagine the ruins you see as complete, tall buildings, and the whole settlement as a place where monks prayed and worked for centuries. It is remarkable, too, to think that men made such huge and fine buildings so long ago, not thinking of how much they would be paid but of how good a job they could make.

Something for You to Do

1. Why did some men choose to become monks? What were their two main duties?
2. Draw a plan of Melrose Abbey.
3. Make a list of the main parts of the abbey, and explain what each was used for.
4. How did the abbey benefit (a) the monks, (b) the people, and (c) the country?
5. Imagine that you live in the country in the Middle Ages, and that a band of monks come to build an abbey nearby. Write a paragraph showing what you think about their arrival and their work.
6. In David I's reign, the monks at Melrose fed 4000 starving people during three months of famine. Write a short play about this, and the class can act it.

Chapter 15

THE STRUGGLE FOR INDEPENDENCE

1. *Under William Wallace*

In the end, my friends,
We've nane but the folk; they've nocht
To loss but life and libertie
But gin we've thame, we've aa. They're Scotland
Nane ither.

Sydney Goodsir Smith: *The Wallace*

The life of the ordinary man in the touns of Scotland strikes us as humdrum and hopeless, but it was relieved by the occasional holiday (holy day), and by the hope of a happier life in Heaven. Though he might not notice it in the reign of Alexander III (1249-86), his country was becoming prosperous. The king's laws were observed, and his hold on the land was firm. More burghs were founded, and trade increased, especially by way of the port of Berwick. More and more serfs were gaining their freedom. Agriculture was flourishing under the guiding hand of the monks. The Vikings, defeated at *Largs* in 1263 by storms, disease, and Alexander's forces, agreed to return the Hebrides to Scotland and to leave the country alone. Scotland was at peace with her southern neighbour. It was an age of peace and prosperity —a 'golden age'.

The discovery of the king's dead body below the cliffs at Kinghorn in 1286 brought this happy period in our history to a sudden end. He left no son to succeed him; the heiress was a young girl—Margaret, the 'Maid of Norway'. When she died in Orkney, Scotland had a difficult problem of succession on her hands. The contenders for the Crown

might have gathered support and waged war against each other to establish their claims. Instead, they asked Edward I of England to decide who should be king.

Edward had recently conquered the Welsh and built strong castles to keep the peace in Wales, and he dreamed of the whole island being brought under his control. First, he insisted on being recognised as overlord of Scotland, and then, by the *Award of Berwick*, he gave the throne to John Balliol—a weak man who could be 'managed' but who did have the best claim.

John Balliol as King

King John ruled like a puppet, and his overlord pulled the strings. Edward interfered at every opportunity to show his authority, even summoning John to England to pay a wine bill owed by Alexander III. When he demanded that the Scots should provide men and money for an English war against France, Edward went too far. Scotsmen had never been forced to fight abroad even for their own king, and now a council of barons insisted on an alliance with France against their common enemy, Edward I of England. This Franco-Scottish alliance of 1295, later called the *Auld Alliance*, was to influence both countries, drawing them together and involving Scotland in wars against England until the time of Mary Queen of Scots.

A Scottish raid on the north of England drew the full force of Edward's anger. With a well-equipped army, he captured Berwick and put all the inhabitants to the sword, until the streets streamed with blood. At Dunbar, the Scottish army was defeated, and Balliol soon had to surrender to his English overlord. Edward subdued the land as far north as Elgin. English nobles took charge of the country, and English troops occupied the castles. The Stone of Destiny was removed from Scone, the crowning place of Scottish kings, to be set in the coronation chair in Westminster Abbey, while the Holy Rood of St. Margaret, said to be part of Christ's Cross, and the bulk of the Scottish records of state, were taken south. Edward's control of Scotland appeared to be complete.

The Fight for Freedom

Although most of the nobles swore an oath of homage to Edward, few of the people welcomed the English soldiers or were willing to pay taxes to the English. The nation's hour of need produced the leaders it required. 'Ane nobil young man, callit William Wallace inspyrit by God,' a Scottish writer tells us, 'tuik pairt with the puir pepill and defendit the realm.' Wallace was not one of the great nobles, but a knight's son from Elderslie in Renfrewshire. He had reason to hate the English. After he had slain an English soldier in a quarrel they killed his wife in Lanark and burned his house. In his fury Wallace led a raid against the English in Lanark and killed Hazelrig, the English sheriff, with his own sword. News of this exploit kindled the spirit of rebellion. His band of followers became an army as the

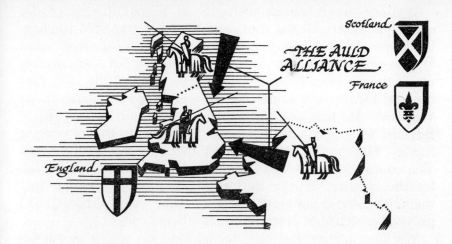

common folk flocked to join him. He was a local hero, soon to become a great patriot determined to free his country from the invaders. But a man who is a hero to his fellow-countrymen may be regarded quite differently by his enemies. The monks in a priory just south of the Border recorded this opinion in their chronicle:

'A certain bloody man, William Wallace, who before that had been the leading bandit in Scotland . . . induced the poor people to gather to his aid.'

Meanwhile another knight's son, Andrew of Moray, was driving the English garrisons out of the castles in the north. When Wallace was attacking Dundee in 1297, he heard that an English army was marching north towards Stirling. Joined by Andrew of Moray and his men, he made for Stirling and waited in a strong position covering the wooden bridge across the Forth. Foolishly the English began to cross the narrow bridge. When about half the English army was over, and waiting to re-form its ranks, Wallace sounded his horn for the attack. The Scots charged, and captured the end of the bridge. The English could not retreat or be reinforced. They perished on the field of battle or in the river, while the remainder, unwilling spectators on the south bank, turned and fled.

Wallace drove the English out of the south-east of the country. Scotland was free, and Wallace was able to show his authority by inviting the merchants of Lubeck and Hamburg to come and trade here again. But the country was suffering from famine, because so much of the land had been laid waste and so many men were away, fighting under Wallace. He led an expedition into England, which drove Edward to collect another army and pursue the retreating Scots. He caught and defeated them at *Falkirk* in 1298. The courage and spears of the Scottish army were no match for the cavalry charges and showers of arrows which met them. Scotland suffered a serious defeat, and Edward had proved himself the 'Hammer of the Scots'.

Wallace, having lost the battle, kept on trying to set his country free. English troops were everywhere, attempting to put down local risings. It seemed to Edward that his grip on Scotland would not be secure until Wallace was his prisoner. At last Wallace was tricked by Sir John Menteith, a Scottish knight who had submitted to the English king. He was taken prisoner at Robroyston near Glasgow, and handed over to Edward. He was taken to London, tried for treason to a king he did not recognise, and condemned to a horrible death. He died for Scotland.

Something for You to Do

1. Why has the reign of Alexander III been called 'The Golden Age of Scottish History'?
2. What happened after the death of Alexander III? Start with the death of the Maid of Norway, and make a list of events in order. Keep asking youself 'what happened next?'
3. Read again the two opinions of William Wallace. What do you think of him?
4. Make a map of central Scotland and insert the places mentioned in the chapter. Use signs like ✗ = 'Battle'.
5. Imagine that you are a war correspondent of a newspaper. Write an eye-witness account of the Battle of Stirling.

Chapter 16

THE STRUGGLE FOR INDEPENDENCE

2. *Under Robert the Bruce*

Ah Freedom is a noble thing!
Freedom makes man to have liking;[1]
Freedom all solace to man gives;
He lives at ease that freely lives!

John Barbour: *The Brus*

Any hope of Scotland regaining her freedom must have died almost completely when news came that Wallace was dead. English soldiers living in every castle and burgh were signs to the Scottish people that Edward was their lord. The land was bare, and food was scarce. But within a year the Scots had a new leader, a man of rank who was prepared to give up his English lands to fight for Scotland's freedom. He was descended from the Norman to whom David I had given Annandale, and he had a strong right to be king. His name was Robert the Bruce.

To rid Scotland of the English was difficult enough, but Bruce added to his difficulties. In 1306, at the Grey Friars' Church in Dumfries, he met his rival for the crown—John Comyn, the 'Red Comyn'. They quarrelled, Bruce wounded Comyn with his dagger and, as he rushed out to confess that he had disturbed the peace of a holy place, his friends went in and killed the wounded man. Comyn's men became his deadly foes, and the Church regarded him as a murderer and an enemy of God.

When he was crowned at Scone, the ceremony took place in secret, although the Bishops of Glasgow and St. Andrews did attend in spite of the ban of the Church on Bruce.

[1] *Liking*: pleasure.

91

Robert the Bruce might now call himself Robert I, King of Scotland, but he was a king hunted in his own country. A defeat by the English in Methven Wood near Perth was followed by another in the west at the hands of the Red Comyn's relatives. He was forced to leave the mainland altogether for a time. When he returned to Ayrshire with a small band of desperate men, he adopted the tactics of a guerilla fighter—to raid, to ambush, to harass the enemy, but to avoid open battles against larger numbers than his own. He and his men 'lived off the land'. They carried only little bags of oatmeal to make oatcakes; they hunted deer and killed cattle and sheep to feed themselves. The death of Edward I, the 'Hammer of the Scots', made Bruce's task easier because his son, Edward II, was not a soldier of his father's quality, and preferred living in his court in England to campaigning in Scotland. This gave Bruce the opportunity, which he grasped, of dealing with his Scottish enemies. Galloway, Aberdeenshire, and Argyll—'the Comyn counties'—were conquered, and the north of Scotland was now strongly behind him.

At last Bruce could turn his attention to his English foes, the soldiers holding the Scottish castles. Though he took many of the smaller towers quite easily, he lacked the heavy siege-engines which were necessary to capture castles by direct attack. He had to use his eyes to detect weaknesses in the defence, and his wits to trick the enemy. Often his men scaled walls by using rope ladders with hooks, which could be uplifted on the points of their spears to catch the top of a castle wall. Perth was captured by Bruce's men wading across the moat in winter up to the neck in water; Linlithgow by men hidden under a load of hay; Roxburgh by Sir James Douglas's men wearing dark cloaks and being mistaken for cattle; Edinburgh Castle by Sir Thomas Randolph's men who daringly climbed the cliffs of the castle rock. The capture of these castles makes thrilling reading, and you can find all the stories in Sir Walter Scott's *Tales of a Grandfather* or H. W. Meikle's *Story of Scotland*.

Edward II's hold on Scotland was now slender. Only the castles at Bothwell and Stirling held out for him. He was forced to march north at once, and set out with a splendid army, the largest to invade Scotland up to that time. 20,000 men there were, raising the dust on the road north to Stirling, their main strength lying in the long column of heavily-armoured knights on horseback. The Scots had only 6000 men, including only a few horsemen and archers. When the Scottish scouts surveyed the enemy and picked out the longbowmen and plumed horsemen, they must have wondered, 'Will this be a defeat like Falkirk, all over again?'

The Battle of Bannockburn, 1314

But Bruce had chosen his position well on the wooded ground of New Park. Protected to the south by the bog, and by the pits which his men had dug near the Bannock Burn as traps for the English horses, Bruce blocked the road to Stirling Castle. Edward must either attack the Scots in the wood, where his cavalry would be hampered, or else take the low road across the marsh between New Park and the Forth. On the afternoon of the 23rd June, the English cavalry tried a direct attack on the Scots in the wood, but some floundered in the pits and the rest withdrew. The English knight, De Bohun, charging at the king, was felled at the cost of the king's good battle-axe.

Edward's army crossed the Bannock and camped for the night, facing the Scottish position and with the Bannock and the Forth behind. They were in a trap. When the sun came up, columns of Scottish spearmen advanced boldly down the slope. They stopped and knelt in prayer.

The Battle of BANNOCKBURN

'See,' said Edward, 'they kneel to ask for mercy.'

'Yes, sire, but not from you,' said a knight near him. 'It is God's mercy that they seek. These men will conquer or die.'

Edward could not believe it. Here came Scottish foot-soldiers in columns, their spears thrust out like the prickles of a hedgehog, daring to attack English knights and bowmen. A counter-attack by the English cavalry crumbled before the Scottish spears; a word from Bruce and his horsemen routed the archers; this certainly was to be no repetition of the battle of Falkirk. But the battle was not yet won. The English were superior in equipment and men, but they had no room to deploy their forces. The fighting was desperate, hand-to-hand. You could hear the clang of sword on armour, the splintering of wood, the mad gallop of riderless horses, the shouting, the moans of dying men. The battle was confused, but the English were trapped with water at their backs.

Probably by Bruce's orders, the 'small folk', the armed farmers and camp-followers, left their shelter in the valley for the field of battle.

'On them,' they shouted, 'On them! They fail!' Their arrival encouraged the Scots; they seemed like a fresh army to the English, who broke and fled. The Forth swallowed many an English knight. An early writer tells us that, 'Bannockburn of horses and men so charged was, that upon drowned horses and men, men might pass dry over it.'

The battle of Bannockburn, on the 24th June 1314, was Scotland's greatest victory. Much booty was taken, and the English surrendered Stirling Castle. Fighting continued for several years in the form of raids into the north of England, until independence was won and admitted by the English by the *Treaty of Northampton* in 1328. Scotland was a free nation.

What Scotland fought for is best described in the noble letter to the Pope in 1320, known as the *Declaration of Arbroath*, which asked him to recognise Robert I as king of an independent Scotland.

> For so long as one hundred men remain alive, we shall never under any conditions submit to the domination of the English. It is not for glory or riches or honour that we fight, but only for liberty, which no good man will consent to lose but with his life.

Bruce's Heart

Bruce had saved Scotland, but could he save his own soul? As long as the ban of the Church was on him, he was denied a Christian burial, and believed he had no prospect of reaching Heaven. At length, worn down by his labours and stricken by incurable leprosy, he heard the good news that the Pope recognised him as king and as a faithful member of the Church. He was too ill to go on the crusade on which he had always set his heart, but he made Sir James Douglas, 'the good Sir James', promise to carry his heart, enclosed in a casket, to the Holy Land after his death.

For the past two hundred years, Christian knights of many lands had fought in the Crusades or 'Wars of the Cross', to free Palestine from the Mohammedan Turks who had conquered it. Few Scots had gone there to fight, because of the constant danger to their own country from England. Sir James Douglas and his companions, however, set out and fought against the Mohammedans in Spain. There, in the thick of the battle, Douglas and his followers perished. Bruce's heart was returned safely to Scotland and placed in Melrose Abbey.

Something for You to Do

1. Start with the murder of the Red Comyn in 1306, and ask yourself, 'What happened next?' Make a list of the main events that occurred in Bruce's lifetime.
2. Fill in the places mentioned in this chapter on the map which you drew for the chapter before it. Use the sign ♖ to mean 'Castle '.
3. What were the reasons for the Scottish victory at Bannockburn?
4. Copy carefully the quotation from the Declaration of Arbroath into your note-book. The words are worth learning.
5. Which of the castles captured by Bruce's men is nearest to your home? Read the full account of its capture.
6. For an 'eye-witness account' of Bannockburn, read *I was at Bannockburn*, by Agnes Mure Mackenzie.
7. Find out more about the Crusades. Look up an encyclopaedia and read the articles on: Mohammed, Mohammedanism, the Koran, Richard I, Saladin. A good story about the Crusades is *Knight Crusader*, by Ronald Welch.

Chapter 17

SCOTLAND IN THE LATER MIDDLE AGES

> This is my country,
> The land that begat me.
> These windy spaces
> Are surely my own,
> And those who here toil
> In the sweat of their faces
> Are flesh of my flesh
> And bone of my bone.
>
> Sir Alexander Gray: *Scotland*

The Wars of Independence were Scotland's moment of glory. Invasion and battle welded her people into a nation, but the price of victory was heavy. Scotland had strained to win against a great and wealthy neighbour, and most of the battles had been fought on her own soil. People and beasts, burghs and touns, castles and kirks, had suffered heavily, and the men who fought for Bruce had to return to rebuild what had been cast down.

We do not know how many people there were in Scotland then. Probably they numbered about 400,000 in Bruce's time—less than the population of Edinburgh to-day. Famine and fighting always kept the population low, but in 1349-50 a great plague struck the country. This was the *Black Death*, which had already killed millions in Europe. It spread from England into Scotland, where people called it 'the Foul Death of the English'. Great numbers of people in Scotland died, perhaps as many as 100,000, or one person out of every four.

Defending the Realm

What the country needed after the Wars of Independence was a period of peace and of firm but kindly government. She gained neither.   When Robert the Bruce died, he was succeeded by his five-year-old son, David II.   England under Edward III continued to be the 'Auld Enemy', and defeated the Scots almost at will.

Edward marched north in the hope of capturing Berwick, Scotland's busiest seaport.   In 1333, his archers slaughtered the Scottish army at the battle of *Halidon Hill*.   Berwick became English for a time, and soon Scotland was ravaged by fire and sword as she had been in the time of William Wallace.   Towns as far north as Elgin and Aberdeen were burned, and some of the castles which Bruce's men had destroyed were repaired and filled with English troops.

No great Scottish patriot rose up to lead a national revolt against the invaders, but a woman defied them.   She was the Countess of March (also known as 'Black Agnes'), the daughter of Sir Thomas Randolph, who had been one of Bruce's lieutenants at Bannockburn.   She held the castle of Dunbar successfully against an English siege.   When stones

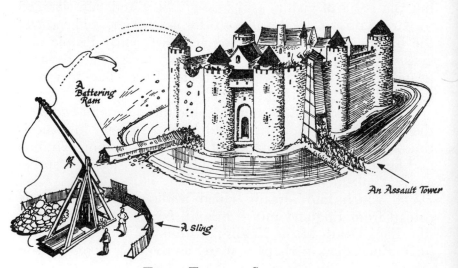

THREE TYPES OF SEIGE-ENGINE

were hurled at the walls by the English siege-engines, she and her maids went out with cloths to wipe away the dust. As the months passed, food became so scarce in the castle that it seemed that the defenders would have to surrender. But a brave Scot, Alexander Ramsay, saved them by bringing food by night from the Bass Rock. Black Agnes mockingly sent some white bread and wine as a gift to the English commander, and in disgust he called off the siege.

Fortunately for Scotland, most of Edward's forces were needed elsewhere. In 1339 he attacked France, in what was to become the *Hundred Years War*. The Scots were still obliged by the 'Auld Alliance' to make raids on the north of England. In one raid, they penetrated south of the Tyne, but were defeated at *Neville's Cross* (1346). David II, Bruce's disappointing son, was taken prisoner, and finally released for a ransom of over £65,000—a crippling sum for a poor country.

Robert II, the first of the *Stewart* line, became king on the death of David II in 1371. His claim to the throne was sound, for he was the son of Marjory Bruce, the eldest daughter of Robert I. He hoped to remain at peace with England, but 2000 French knights arrived in Scotland to help in a raid against the English. The attack failed, and the enemy came north and burned Edinburgh and the abbeys of Melrose and Dryburgh.

In 1388 the Scots returned to the attack. The Earl of Douglas advanced into the lands of Sir Henry Percy and captured his pennon. Percy gathered his forces, and marched against Douglas at *Otterburn*. The armies fought fiercely by moonlight, with axe and spear, sword and dagger. Three times wounded, Douglas fell, but the English did not know that the Scottish leader was dying. The Scots attacked once more, shouting *'Douglas! Douglas!'* and the English were driven from the field. Douglas died, but won the battle, which had been foretold to him in a dream, as we hear in the old ballad *The Battle of Otterbourne*—

> I saw a dead man win a fight,
> And I think that man was I.

Kings and Barons

Kings of Scotland—1329-1488	
David II: 1329-71	James I: 1406-37
Robert II: 1371-90	James II: 1437-60
Robert III: 1390-1406	James III: 1460-88

After the Wars of Independence, the lands belonging to the barons who had opposed Bruce were taken from them and given as rewards to Bruce's faithful friends. In this way, the families of some of them became very powerful, but there was little danger from great landowners as long as the king was strong and respected by all. After Robert I, however, Scotland was unfortunate in her kings. David II never took firm control; Robert II, the first of the Stewarts, was too old; his son Robert III was kindly but weak; while James I was absent for eighteen years in an English gaol. For almost a century (1329-1424), no king had the soldiers, the money, or the determination to keep the barons in check. The vital link in the feudal chain—fealty to the king—was broken, and the heads of landed families ruled their own areas like independent kings. By bonds of *manrent*, smaller families attached themselves to powerful lords, and the armies which some lords could put in the field were numbered in thousands. In the reign of James II, it was said that the Earl of Douglas had 30,000 men at his command. This was feudalism run wild.

The king's sheriffs were helpless against the local lords. Among the most powerful families were the Crawfords, the Gordons, the Ogilvies, the Lindsays, the Hamiltons, and the Homes. In the south-west,

> Frae Wigton to the toon o' Ayr
> Port Patrick to the Cruives o' Cree,
> Nae man wad think to bide there
> Unless he coort wi' Kennedy.

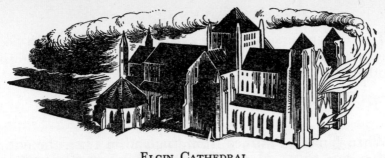

ELGIN CATHEDRAL
Burned in 1390

Keeping Scotland in order proved to be beyond the powers of Robert III. As soon as this gentle, crippled man became king in 1390, his own brother the 'Wolf of Badenoch' came out from his lair at Loch-an-Eilean and raided the lands of the Bishop of Moray. With a band of 'wild wikkit hielandmen', he looted and burned the cathedral of Elgin.

Clan fought against clan, sometimes for honour, sometimes to settle who owned a piece of grazing land. The king could do nothing to stop them. At a clan fight in Perth, Robert III was a helpless spectator as thirty champions from each of the two clans Chattan and Kay fought each other with axe, sword, and dagger until nearly all were slain.

Such troubled times drove the king to send his son James to France for safety, but the boy might have been safer at home. His ship was captured by the English, and he was held prisoner in England.

During his absence in England, his father died, and the government was carried on by *regents*. Their task was made harder by the ambitious Lord of the Isles. He was master of all the lands in the west from Kintyre to Lewis, a greater area than the Vikings had controlled, and he made treaties with England as if he had been an independent prince. In 1411 Donald, the second Lord of the Isles, claimed the earldom of Ross and advanced on Aberdeen. In a fierce battle at *Harlaw*, his Highlanders were defeated by the spearmen of Buchan and Angus under the Earl of Mar, helped by burgesses from Aberdeen.

> And Hieland and Lowland may mournful be
> For the sair field of Harlaw.

The town was saved, but the battle shows how much Scotland needed a king who could keep one baron from fighting another.

Kings Who Tried Hard

JAMES I

When James I returned from England in 1424, the nation had such a king. He was manly and intelligent, and saw that it was his duty to restore order in Scotland and make her prosperous. He called Parliaments,[1] which representatives of the Church and burghs attended together with the barons. Parliament became his ally by passing laws to maintain peace in the land. Every man was ordered to be properly armed according to his rank, and to become skilled in archery in case of war. Barons were not to ride about the country with bands of armed followers, or to make private wars on one another.

James acted swiftly, perhaps too swiftly, against his 'overmighty subjects'. His cousin the Duke of Albany, who had been regent during the king's imprisonment in England, was captured and executed at Stirling. In 1427 Parliament was summoned to meet at Inverness and the Highland chiefs were ordered to attend. Forty of them were immediately arrested and imprisoned, and the most dangerous were put to death.

James's ruthless methods aroused opposition, and some of the nobles plotted against him. When he was staying at Perth in 1437, he was warned that he was in danger but paid no attention. One evening, when he was talking with the queen and her ladies, the clink of weapons was heard outside. James was unarmed, and the bar for the door had disappeared. One of the queen's attendants, Katharine Douglas, used her arm to bar the door while the king escaped through the floorboards to the drains below. Her arm was broken as the assassins burst in. The king was nowhere to be found and the plotters departed. Something, perhaps a noise, called them back. They noticed the loose

---

[1] 'Parliament' comes from the French word *parler*—'to speak'.

boards and plunged down.   The king was trapped and murdered.

JAMES II

James I, like Robert the Bruce, was followed by a child. James II was only six when he became king, and the barons were free to plunge the country into disorder. They even struggled to secure custody of the boy-king. The most powerful baron was the young Earl of Douglas. It was said that he travelled about his lands accompanied by 1000 horsemen. The king's guardians, Crichton and Livingstone, asked Douglas and his brother to come to Edinburgh to visit the king. They arrived and were entertained. Then the head of a black bull was placed on the table. It was a sign of death. Despite young James's protests, his guests were hustled off and executed.

When James II reached manhood, he followed his father's policy, guided by the statesmanlike Bishop Kennedy of St. Andrews. He had the support of Parliament and the Church, but he could not be a real king until he had proved himself stronger than the Douglas family. He discovered that the new Earl of Douglas had formed an alliance against him with other barons, including the Lord of the Isles. Douglas was summoned to meet the king at Stirling Castle, with the promise that no harm would come to him. James told him bluntly that the league of barons must be broken up at once. When Douglas defied him, James drew a dagger and stabbed him. James's action stung the Douglasses into rebellion. On Kennedy's advice, the king proceeded against Douglas's allies one by one. Then he advanced into the Douglas territory, destroying castles and laying waste the land. The power of the Douglasses was at an end. The king was mightier than any baron.

James II's reign ended in tragedy. He determined to win back Roxburgh Castle, which had been held by the English for a century. As James was watching one of his cannon being fired during the assault, it blew up and killed him.

JAMES III

Once again the new king was only a boy, but James III had Bishop Kennedy to advise him. In 1469, he married Margaret of Scandinavia, and when her dowry was not paid Orkney and Shetland passed to the Scottish Crown.

James III was clever and businesslike. He shunned the company of the nobles, preferring to have talented men around him such as Cochran, the architect who built the Great Hall at Stirling Castle. The barons were jealous of the new men. When the king's army camped at Lauder, on its way to defend Berwick against an English attack, the barons decided to take action against the favourites. Cochran and the others were arrested and hanged over Lauder Bridge. No Scottish army marched to save Berwick, which has been an English town ever since.

James was challenged, as his father and grandfather had been, by barons who combined against him. They captured his son Prince James, and made him their king. In 1488, father and son faced each other in battle at *Sauchieburn* near Stirling. James III was thrown from his horse and carried to a corn mill where, thinking that he was going to die, he asked for a priest. He was stabbed by a dagger in an unknown hand.

Something for You to Do

1. What were the effects of the Wars of Independence on Scotland?
2. Explain carefully: the 'Auld Alliance', ransom, manrent, the Lordship of the Isles, Parliament, 'overmighty subjects'.
3. Which family was powerful in your district at this time? Is one of its castles or towers still standing? Find out all you can about it.
4. Make a map of Scotland, showing the places mentioned in this chapter. Call it *Scotland in the later Middle Ages*.
5. Make a time chart for Scotland for the period 1329-1488, showing the rulers and main events.

Chapter 18

THE AGE OF DISCOVERY

When does a boy become a youth? When does a youth become a man? It is impossible to say exactly. In the same way, we know that one age in history differs from the age before it, but we cannot say exactly when the new age begins.

The Middle Ages was that period in history when the Pope was recognised as God's representative on earth by every Christian in western Europe. Everyone looked to Rome for guidance. Inside each country, a man's position depended on the land he held. Thus, the priest in his church and the lord in his castle were the two great authorities whom everyone believed and obeyed. But churchmen were the only educated men, and, as we might expect, their studies were completely concerned with religion. 'What do the scholars say?' people asked. 'These things we must learn and believe.'

In the fifteenth century, the modern age dawned in the minds of men. They were no longer satisfied with what some authority told them to believe. They began to ask questions, not about the next world but about the world around them. They became curious about its shape and its size, and about the stars and the planets. They wanted to test, to experiment, to prove things for themselves. To find the truth became a quest—it was the real way to learn. This new age was called the *Renaissance*, meaning the rebirth of enthusiasm for learning.

The Renaissance began in Italy, in cities like Florence and Venice where merchants came into contact with the ideas of foreign lands in the course of trade. The people in Italy could see around them ruins which reminded them of the civilisation of ancient Rome. Perhaps, the scholars thought, thinkers in earlier ages had known more about the world than they did. Gradually, manuscripts written in Greek were brought to Italy where they were eagerly studied. This trickle of documents became a flood when the Turks captured Constantinople in 1453. Greek scholars who lived there sought refuge in the West. Many of them settled in Italy and brought their valuable manuscripts with them.

As early as the thirteenth century, Roger Bacon knew about gunpowder, which, when used in pistols and cannon, was to blast the armoured knight and the castle from the thoughts of military men. A king with all the artillery at his command need no longer fear disloyal barons. Copernicus discovered that the earth was not fixed but moved round the sun. Galileo, the Italian scientist, invented the thermometer and first used the telescope to support the ideas of Copernicus. Dropping stones of different sizes from the top of the leaning tower of Pisa, he proved that falling bodies fall at the same rate irrespective of their weight. Leonardo da Vinci, artist, architect, town-planner, sculptor, and engineer—perhaps the man of greatest all-round ability—foresaw the aeroplane and the 'covered chariot'—the tank.

In the Middle Ages, students were in the habit of travelling from place to place to study under great teachers in the universities. Now they were attracted to Italy to study Greek. When they returned home, they carried their enthusiasm for knowledge to Germany, France, the Netherlands, and Britain.

In Germany, the printing press was invented by John Gutenberg, and in 1476 William Caxton set up his press in England. Following the discovery by the Arabs of a cheap way of making paper, it became possible to produce books in large numbers. By the year 1500, there were already nine million books in Europe, compared with about 100,000 manuscripts in the Middle Ages. More people learned to read and write, and so to find things out for themselves.

Men felt the urge to create. There were great artists, such as Leonardo da Vinci, who painted the 'Mona Lisa', and Holbein, whose portraits of Henry VIII of England and of other kings tell us as much about their character as about their appearance. There were architects who went back to the Greeks for inspiration, aiming at a sense of proportion, preferring the lintelled doorway to the medieval arch, and introducing pillars and domes into their buildings.

DETAILS OF RENAISSANCE BUILDING

St. Peter's Church in Rome, and St. Paul's Cathedral, rebuilt in the seventeenth century by Sir Christopher Wren, show these new features. Gradually, poets in every country gave up writing Latin verses and wrote in their own languages.

ROUTES OF THE GREAT DISCOVERERS

Voyages of Discovery

People became inquisitive about other lands. The world they knew in the Middle Ages was small, consisting of Europe and the lands round the Mediterranean, to which Arab traders brought the wealth of the East, from India, China, and the Spice Islands or East Indies. Exploration was possible now that sailors had the compass to guide them.

Prince Henry the Navigator, of Portugal, encouraged his sea-captains to sail farther and farther south along the coast of Africa. Diaz reached the Cape of Good Hope, and Vasco da Gama rounded the Cape, crossed the Indian Ocean, and in 1498 arrived in India. This new route to the East was followed by sailors until the opening of the Suez Canal in 1869.

'If the world is round, why not reach India by sailing westwards?' With this thought in his mind, Christopher Columbus, a sailor from Genoa, set sail in 1492 with three ships provided by Queen Isabella of Spain. Weeks on the open sea terrified his men, but Columbus persuaded them to continue. They reached a group of islands and explored some of them, including Cuba and Haiti. Columbus thought they were the Spice Islands, and called them *Indies*. In later voyages he touched the coast, not of Asia as he imagined, but of South America. Other captains followed. John Cabot claimed Newfoundland for England. Amerigo Vespucci, who gave America its name, explored the coast of South America. Balboa crossed the land of Panama and saw the Pacific Ocean.

But they had not reached India by sailing west.

In 1519, Ferdinand Magellan sailed from Spain with five ships to solve the problem. Trying to find a way round South America, he penetrated the straits which bear his name and entered the Pacific Ocean. Months of hunger and weary sailing brought him to the East Indies. Magellan was killed but the voyage went on, across the Indian Ocean and round the Cape of Good Hope until one ship and eighteen men reached Spain. Their route to the East Indies was too long to be of value to sailors, but they had proved that the world was round.

These were exciting times, as exciting as our own. Adventurers returned with gold and silver, black men, and strange stories. They had conquered the oceans as we have conquered the air. A new continent, America, had appeared over the western seas, and the countries facing the Atlantic— Spain, Portugal, France, and England—were well placed to become wealthy by trade.

Scotland under James IV (1488-1513)

What was Scotland's position in this new age? The country produced no outstanding artists, scientists, or explorers. It stood on the fringe of the great changes that were taking place in Europe. At the court, the king was determined that his country should not be out-of-date. James IV was a great all-rounder—a superb athlete and horseman, a keen scientist and surgeon, and a scholar who knew Latin and Gaelic and five foreign languages.

He made sure that peace prevailed in his kingdom. He sailed with his fleet to the Western Isles and broke the power of the Lord of the Isles. More sheriffs were set over the Highlanders. Anxious to know what was going on in his kingdom, James was always on the move. He made tours in person to see conditions for himself, and to make sure that justice was being done.

He showed concern for education. His own son studied under the great Dutch scholar Erasmus. Scotland already had two universities—St. Andrews and Glasgow—and James IV founded the third at Aberdeen in 1495, to produce lawyers and, for the first time in Britain, to train doctors as well. A few years later, the craft of surgery was recognised in Edinburgh, and no man was allowed to practise unless he was qualified. In 1496, barons and freeholders were ordered to send their eldest sons to grammar schools at the age of eight or nine, until they had 'perfect Latin and understanding of the laws'. Here for the first time was education for boys who did not intend to become churchmen.

In 1508 the printing of books began. In their shop in
Edinburgh, Walter Chapman and Andrew Millar published
their first volume, which included poems by William Dunbar,
who wrote *The Thistle and the Rose* to celebrate the wedding
of James to Margaret Tudor of England. Dunbar, a
wandering scholar who became one of the king's clerks, was
a poet of outstanding merit. He and the other poets of his
day wrote, not in the medieval Latin of the scholars, but in
the language of their own people. Gavin Douglas in fact
translated the works of Latin poets like Virgil and Horace
into 'the braid Scots'. It was a Dunfermline schoolmaster,
Robert Henryson, who told fascinating stories about animals
in his *Moral Fables*. What do you think of his description
of the worried little mouse in these lines?

> Ane lytill mous come till ane Rever syde;
> Scho micht not waid, hir schankis wer sa short,
> Scho culd not swym, scho had na hors to ryde;
> Of verray force behovit her to byde,
> And to and fra besyde the Rever deip
> Scho ran, cryand with mony pietuous peip.

James IV was curious about scientific discoveries. He
bought books and chemicals, and carried out experiments on
his own, but was taken in by one John Damian, a foreign
impostor who claimed that he could turn other metals into
gold. Damian even tried to become the first man to fly.
Wearing wings made of feathers, he leapt from the walls of
Stirling Castle,

> And in the myre, up till the een,
> Among the glaur did glyde,

according to Dunbar, who made fun of Damian's efforts.

James encouraged shipbuilding in Scotland. He ordered
burghs on the coast to build small ships for fishing. When
English pirates interfered with Scottish trading vessels in the
Firth of Forth, Sir Andrew Wood of Largo in Fife went out
with two ships—the *Flower* and the *Yellow Carvel*—to fight
them. After a desperate battle, he captured the five English
ships.

THE 'GREAT MICHAEL'

Realising the need for sea-power, James brought ship-wrights over from France and the Netherlands. In the royal dockyard at Newhaven near Leith they built stout ships, including the *Great Michael*, the biggest ship of her day. To build her, men 'cut down all the woods of Fife, except Falkland Wood, in addition to all the timber that was brought out of Norway'. Measuring 250 feet from stem to stern, she was armed with more than 300 guns and cost £30,000. At sea, Scotland became a power to be reckoned with.

When English troops were fighting against the French in 1513, James declared war on Henry VIII of England. As his forces from all over Scotland rallied to him, he advanced over the Border. Wark and Norham castles fell to his artillery. He took up such a strong position on Flodden Hill that the Earl of Surrey, the English commander, dared not attack him. Surrey led his men round the Scottish flank and placed them between the Scots and Scotland. Under cover of smoke the Scots turned to face them. The English artillery out-gunned the Scots, and its accurate fire tore great gaps in the Scottish ranks. The battle was fought on foot, but the Scots, armed with fifteen-foot pikes, lost formation as they crossed the rough ground. These awkward weapons were useless at close quarters against the English halberds or bills, which, with eight-foot shafts, could be used both as spears and battle-axes. James, who fought in front, had his pike shattered, and was killed only a pike's length from the Earl of Surrey. In the hand-to-hand battle that followed, the Scots could not reach the English bill-men with their swords. The Scots 'could not resist the bills that lighted so thick and so sore upon them', and thousands were killed.

It was more a massacre than a battle. Though the Scots were

superior in numbers, guns, and food-supplies, they were a feudal host compared with this English army of professional soldiers, disciplined and armed with a weapon to which the Scots had no answer. Scotland was not as modern as she had thought.

Something for You to Do

1. Under the heading *They Began the Modern Age*, make notes on: (*a*) Scientists; (*b*) Printers; (*c*) Artists; (*d*) Explorers. Use an encyclopaedia to find out more about them. The book *Beyond the Sunset*, by Boog-Watson and Carruthers, has stories of the voyages of exploration.
2. Explain how the following discoveries changed men's lives: Gunpowder; the Compass; Printing; the Telescope; America.
3. Which event would you choose as the beginning of the modern age, and why?
4. Make a map of the voyages of discovery, using a different colour or sign for each explorer's route.
5. Write down three ways in which James IV encouraged learning.
6. Explain why the Scots were so heavily defeated at Flodden.
7. Read Jean Elliot's version of *The Flowers of the Forest*.

Chapter 19

CHANGES IN RELIGION

1. *Scotland, England, and the Continent*

In most towns there are at least two places of worship, the Church of Scotland and the Roman Catholic Church, because nowadays Christians do not all agree on what they believe or on how they should worship. People are now free to worship how and where they please. Until the sixteenth century, however, everyone in western Europe was a member of the same Church—the Roman Catholic Church. Every town and parish had its priest, and the local church was the place of worship for everybody. Why and how, then, did people divide and become members of different Churches?

As we saw in Chapter 14, kings and nobles gave much land to the Church, until it became extremely wealthy. In Scotland in the sixteenth century, the annual income of the Church amounted to £300,000, while the king never had more than £45,000 a year from all sources. The king and the nobles envied the Church its great wealth, and wanted to share it. James IV's son, for example, became Archbishop of St. Andrews when he was only eleven years old, so that he might have the income attached to that high position. Nobles had themselves appointed *commendators* (guardians) of bishoprics and abbeys to gain money for themselves. Such appointments did nothing to help the Church in its work.

When the abbeys became rich, they began to attract the wrong type of man. Some men entered an abbey because it was now a comfortable life. In the early fifteenth century, for example, it was recorded that each monk at Melrose

Abbey had a private garden, in spite of the rule which forbade monks to have any private property.

The people even began to look on the parish priest as an enemy. They had to pay him an early kind of death duty:

> Our vicar took the best cow by the heid
> Within an hour, when my father was deid.
> And when the vicar heard tell how that my mother
> Was deid, frae hand he took frae me another.[1]

They also paid a *tithe* or tenth of all their flocks and crops to keep the priest and to help the poor folk of the parish. But by 1560 half the parishes in Scotland had been taken over by the abbeys, which collected all the dues and sent someone —often an ignorant stranger—to preach to the people occasionally. Many priests had given up preaching. One law ordered them to preach at least four times a year, and a later one to preach 'as often as they can do so conveniently'. Some priests could recite the service in Latin but did not understand it. When the Archbishop of St. Andrews issued a new *Catechism in the Scottish Tongue*, he ordered the priests to rehearse it so that they would not stammer and be laughed at by the congregation.

Printing, too, played its part. William Tyndale's translation of the Bible into English was published, and traders brought copies back with them to Scotland. When people, and especially scholars, studied the Gospel they found fault with some things that the priests were teaching.

The Reformation in Europe

Martin Luther, a German professor, was the first to raise his voice in anger. Hearing that a friar was selling 'pardons' for sins, even for sins committed by dead relatives, his conscience rebelled. He felt that a man would be forgiven if he were truly sorry for his sin. Here he saw his fellow-countrymen paying for what he thought were worthless promises. Hard-earned German money was going to help to build the magnificent Church of St. Peter in Rome. He

[1] Sir David Lindesay: *The Thrie Estatis.*

composed ninety-five arguments against these pardons, and nailed them to the church door in Wittenberg in 1517.

Long discussions followed. Luther broadened his attack to include other faults in the Church and to challenge the authority of the Pope himself. The Pope expelled him from the Church, and the Emperor declared him an outlaw. Luther showed his defiance by burning the Pope's letter in the market place, but he then had to go into hiding. He translated the Bible into German. The hymn he composed, *A Safe Stronghold our God is Still*, had half Germany singing. A law was passed which would have crushed the churches which Luther's followers were setting up. Many of the German princes protested, and were given the name *Protestants*.

Luther had tried to correct a fault in the Church, but he failed to convince the Pope. The movement he started, called the *Reformation*, destroyed the unity of the Church, and divided people into Catholics and Protestants.

What Luther was unable to achieve, the Church began to do for itself. It started to put its own house in order. Its chief reformer was a Spanish soldier, Ignatius Loyola. After being severely wounded in battle, he decided to become a soldier of Christ. He formed a new order, the Society of Jesus, whose members were called *Jesuits*. They started fine schools, and trained priests who went into every land to give the Catholic answers to the new ideas.

Scotland and England

Patrick Hamilton, a Scottish student who had attended several universities in Europe, returned to spread Luther's ideas in Scotland. For his fervent preaching he was burned at the stake in St. Andrews. He became a Protestant martyr, and, as an observer remarked, 'the reek of master Patrick Hamilton infected as many as it blew upon'.

Scotland's king, James V, married a Frenchwoman, Mary of Guise. He bound himself to support both the Church of Rome and the Auld Alliance. In England, on the other hand, King Henry VIII, wishing to rid himself

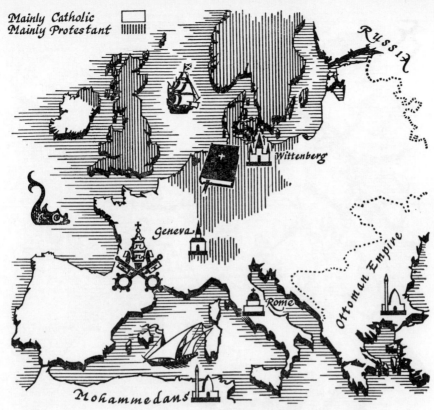

Mainly Catholic
Mainly Protestant

CATHOLIC AND PROTESTANT EUROPE

of his wife, quarrelled with the Pope. He persuaded Parliament to make him head of the Church in England. He closed the monasteries, drove out the monks and took their lands. To prevent Scotland from helping France in a war against England, Henry's army routed the Scots at *Solway Moss* in 1542. James died heart-broken, leaving a new-born girl to become the beautiful but unfortunate Mary Queen of Scots.

Henry suggested a marriage between his son Edward and the child Mary when they were old enough. This far-sighted proposal would have broken Scotland's alliance with France and united the two kingdoms of Scotland and England. When the Scots refused, the English under Hertford invaded.

Central and southern SCOTLAND during the 16th century

Edinburgh was captured, set on fire, and burned for four days. In all, 192 towns, towers, churches, and farmsteads were burned or cast down, and more than 10,000 cattle, 12,000 sheep, and 1000 horses were driven south over the Border. In the next year, 1545, Hertford ruined the Border abbeys in another march of destruction. He returned two years later, to smash another Scottish army at *Pinkie*, near Musselburgh.

This 'Rough Wooing' did not win the hearts of the Scots, and caused Mary to be sent to France to be brought up in safety. But it did urge the Scots on to destroy the old Church. The people learned more about the Word of God as Bibles in English were brought over the Border by the cartload. The Scottish nobles learned how the landowners in England had become rich as the lands taken from the monasteries passed into their hands. Many of them gave support to the Protestants in Scotland, not because they were convinced Protestants but because they wished to gain land.

Persecution continued. The popular Protestant preacher George Wishart took risks in travelling about the country openly to teach his fellow-Scots what he believed. He was arrested, condemned as a heretic, and burned in St. Andrews. Cardinal Beaton, the Catholic leader, was killed in revenge. His assailants, whom John Knox had joined in St. Andrews Castle, were captured after a long siege and sent to France as galley slaves. After nineteen months at the oars, Knox became a minister in the free city of Geneva. He came under the spell of John Calvin, the French Protestant minister who ruled the city. He learned to put his faith in the people rather than in princes and bishops. He saw that Calvin's followers preferred sermons to ceremonies, and worshipped in a church which was plain and undecorated.

In 1559 Knox returned to Scotland.

Something for You to Do

1. (a) Make a list of the exact names of all the churches in your town. Beside each name write the name of the greater church to which each belongs, *e.g.*

   St. Mary's Parish Church—*Church of Scotland.*

   (b) How many are there of each type?
2. Why were many people discontented with the Church before the Reformation?
3. Under the heading *They Made Changes in Religion*, write short notes on William Tyndale, Martin Luther, Ignatius Loyola, Patrick Hamilton, John Calvin.
4. What is the meaning of: *commendator, tithe, Protestant, Jesuit, the Rough Wooing?*
5. On a map of Scotland headed *Changes in Religion*, insert the following places: *St. Andrews, Solway Moss, Edinburgh, Pinkie.*

Chapter 20

CHANGES IN RELIGION

2. *Ministers, Monarchs, and Nobles*

The old Church in Scotland was crumbling. The regent, Mary of Guise, forbade the preaching of the Protestant faith. John Knox preached: it was an act of rebellion. This looming figure with the long face, the black eyebrows, the commanding eyes and flowing black beard thundered against the Church of Rome. He thought it was his duty 'to speik plane, and to flatter no Flesch upon the Face of the Eirth'. The people of Perth, roused by his message, were intent on destruction. They smashed the stained-glass windows and images in the churches of the town. He raised his voice to stop them, but could not control what his own words had set in motion.

The regent saw the need for force. She sought more troops from France, where her daughter Mary was now queen. Knox's main support came from the Protestant lords, who raised what help they could but were not able to match the French in numbers. Maitland of Lethington was sent to ask help from Elizabeth, the Protestant queen of England. She answered by sending an English fleet to the Forth and 9000 men across the Border. Here was a change of policy indeed! English troops were now helping the Scots in battle. The French defended the port of Leith with great skill, but in 1560 the regent died and the garrison surrendered.

1560 proved to be a year of decision. The *Treaty of Edinburgh* [1] forced the French troops to leave Scotland. The Auld Alliance was at an end. No longer would the Scots and French make common cause against the English. The Auld

[1] Sometimes called the *Treaty of Leith*.

Alliance had led to much fighting on the Border, and sent many a Scot to die on fields as disastrous as Flodden. It had kept Scotland in close contact with centres of learning in Europe. Churchmen travelled to and fro, and Scottish students went to study at the University of Paris. French words found their way into Scots—words which we still use to-day, like *fash*, and *runkle* and *ashet*. But Scotland, as she became Protestant, found that she had more in common with her Protestant neighbour England than with the more distant and Catholic France.

John Knox became minister of St. Giles' in Edinburgh. Parliament met and asked the ministers to agree on what they believed. This *Confession of Faith*, as it was called, owed much to the writings of John Calvin. The ministers relied on the Bible for inspiration, and saw 'the preaching of the Word' as their main duty. The Pope's power in Scotland was to end, and Mass was not to be celebrated.

How was the new Church to be organised? Knox provided the answer in his *First Book of Discipline*. The people in each parish were to choose their own minister. Each congregation was to elect elders from its members every year to help to run its Church. Churches in each region were to be supervised by a senior minister called a *superintendent*. The affairs of the Church as a whole were to be discussed every year at a great meeting of ministers and laymen from all over Scotland. This parliament of the Church still meets, and is called the *General Assembly*.

With these ideas the nobles in Parliament agreed, but they could not consent to the wealth of the old Church being taken over by the new.   In fact, many Church lands were already in the hands of the very lords who were sitting in this Parliament.   Because of lack of funds, Knox's bold scheme of education, which would have provided a school in every parish and a college in every town, leading on to the three universities, could not be put into practice.   Scotland missed a great chance of developing a long lead over other countries in education.

Saints' days, the traditional holidays in the Middle Ages, were no longer to be observed.   For those who liked to enjoy themselves, the Reformation wore a solemn face.

Mary Queen of Scots

On a misty morning in 1561, Mary Queen of Scots landed on Scottish soil.   She had succeeded to the throne as an infant, but before the age of six had been sent for safety to her mother's country, France.   She spent many happy years there, and in 1558 married Francis, the heir to the French throne.   A year later Francis and Mary were the rulers of France, but then Francis fell ill and died.   Mary, a widow at eighteen, resolved to return to Scotland.   She was a Catholic, and her northern kingdom had just declared itself Protestant.   On her first Sunday in Holyrood Palace she celebrated Mass, and John Knox declared that this was 'more fearful to him than if ten thousand armed enemies were landed in any part of the realm'.

Even her behaviour was criticised.   Dancing and laughter in Holyrood one evening were sure to be condemned from the pulpit of St. Giles' the next day.   This well-educated, high-spirited, almost foreign queen was sure to need all her courage and charm to deal with scheming lords and a people set against her by the preachings of John Knox.

In religion she remained faithful to the Church of Rome, but undertook to maintain the Protestant Church set up in 1560.   In fact, she led a campaign which put down a rebellion in Aberdeenshire led by the Catholic Earl of Huntly.

This may appear to be a strange policy for a Catholic queen, but Mary's advisers, including Maitland of Lethington,

Mary·Queen of Scots

realised the power of the Protestant lords and ministers. They knew, too, that Mary Tudor had tried to make the English people Catholic again and had failed. Most important of all, Mary hoped that she would one day succeed or replace Elizabeth as queen of England, and so was determined never to disturb the Protestant Church.

Still the Protestants had reason to fear her. She removed a rival by marrying him. He was Lord Darnley, a Catholic who, after herself, was the next heir to the English throne. Plot and murder followed. Darnley was jealous of David Rizzio, the queen's Italian secretary. He was a party to a plot whereby Rizzio was murdered in Holyrood before the queen's eyes.

In 1567, Darnley lay in Kirk o' Field near Edinburgh, so marked with sores that he wore a mask to hide his face. There was an explosion, and 'the hous was raisett up from the ground with pouder'. Darnley was dead. It was discovered that he had been strangled before the explosion. The Earl of Bothwell, the most powerful man in Scotland, was blamed, but he had so many armed men in Edinburgh that his trial was a farce. The queen, who had been nursing her husband, had gone off to Holyrood that evening to attend an entertainment. Had she known about the plot? We do not know, but three months later she married Bothwell.

The Protestant lords turned against them. Mary was imprisoned in Lochleven Castle, where she was forced to abdicate, while Bothwell left Scotland to become a pirate.

In 1568, Mary escaped from her island prison with the help of a boy, young Willie Douglas, who stole the keys of the castle and rowed her to the shore. She gathered some support, but her forces were defeated at *Langside* near Glasgow. There was no hope for her in Scotland now. She took the

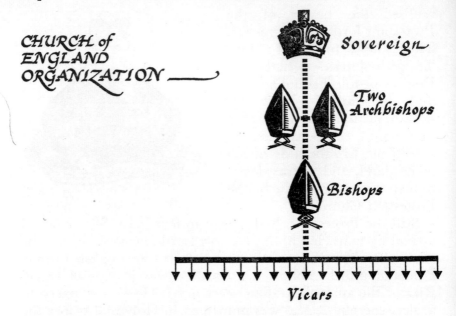

CHURCH of
ENGLAND
ORGANIZATION ———

Sovereign

Two
Archbishops

Bishops

Vicars

risk and fled to England to throw herself at the mercy of her cousin and rival, Queen Elizabeth. She was imprisoned for nearly twenty uncertain years, as English Catholics plotted to take Elizabeth's life and make Mary queen of England. But it was not to be. She was tried at last for having knowledge of a plot, condemned and, as she said, 'delivered from all her cares'.

Andrew Melville and James VI

In Scotland the Protestant Church seemed secure. Knox was preaching with his usual fire. Even when he was so ill that he had to be helped into the pulpit, 'he was so active and vigorous that he was like to ding that pulpit in blads [break it to pieces] and fly out of it'. The king, James VI, was only a child, but he would be a Protestant child, educated by the great Protestant scholar George Buchanan.

What kind of Protestantism was to prevail? Was it to be like that of the Church of England, which had bishops, and the queen as supreme governor?

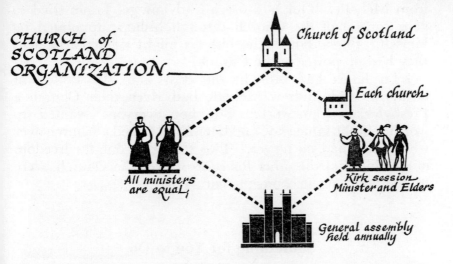

CHURCH of SCOTLAND ORGANIZATION

Church of Scotland

Each church

All ministers are equal

Kirk session Minister and Elders

General assembly held annually

Or was it to be the self-governing Kirk of Scotland that Andrew Melville strove for? After the death of John Knox, this fine scholar spoke for the Kirk. He told the king to his face that there were two kingdoms in Scotland—one the king's, the other Christ's, 'whase subject King James the Saxt is, and of whase kingdome [is] nocht a king nor a lord, nor a heid but a member'. Merchants and craftsmen in the towns gave their support, especially in Dundee, Ayr, St. Andrews, Stirling, Glasgow, and Montrose. Melville triumphed when, in 1592, the Presbyterian Kirk was recognised as the Church of Scotland, with complete control over its own affairs. Believing that ministers should be equal, he denounced the office of superintendent, which reminded him of the medieval bishop. Each kirk was to have its *session* of elders elected for life, and each district its *presbytery*. The policy of the whole Church was to be shaped and controlled by the General Assembly.

James was not yet defeated. The shambling, parentless boy had struggled to become a man. He learned to trust himself and to fear all men. When he rewarded many of the nobles with Church lands they withdrew their support from Melville. Quick to use his advantage, James tried to gain control of the Church through bishops appointed by himself. But although the bishops might sit in Parliament they had no power in the Church.

John Knox had brought the Scots into the Protestant faith; he and Andrew Melville had given their Church a Presbyterian framework. But not everyone wanted to worship in the same way, and later kings feared a Church over which they had no power. Two struggles, one for freedom of worship and the other for control over the Church, were to be fought out in the next century.

Something for You to Do

1. Under the heading *They Made Scotland Protestant*, write notes on: John Knox; Maitland of Lethington; George Buchanan; Andrew Melville.

2. Explain the importance of: the Treaty of Edinburgh; the Auld Alliance; the *First Book of Discipline*; the Battle of Langside.

3. (*a*) Use each of the words *fash*, *runkle*, and *ashet* in a separate sentence, to show that you know what it means.

   (*b*) Try to find English words with the same meanings. Which are the more expressive?

4. Choose a local Presbyterian church. Write down:
   (*a*) its name.
   (*b*) the name of the minister.
   (*c*) the names of as many elders as you can.
   Find out the name of this year's *Moderator* (President) of the General Assembly.

5. On your *Changes in Religion* map insert the following places: *Perth, Lochleven, Langside, Dundee*.

6. The life of Mary Queen of Scots has attracted many authors. In *The Abbot*, Sir Walter Scott describes her escape from Lochleven Castle. An attempt to rescue Mary is the subject of a modern novel—*A Traveller in Time*—by Alison Uttley.

Chapter 21

THE LAND AND THE PEOPLE IN THE SIXTEENTH CENTURY

Four hundred years ago, most of the Scottish people lived in the country and produced nearly everything they needed from the land. Townsmen farmed too, outside the burgh boundaries. To-day, most of us live away from the land and buy our food and clothes in shops. Then, most families lived all their lives in the same place. Roads were few, and people seldom travelled. To-day, we travel by bus or train to work, or on our holidays, or to see a football match. Then, poor people's houses were mainly shelters from the weather and had little furniture in them. The modern 'council house' is better equipped for the enjoyment of life than the laird's tower was in the sixteenth century. Then, news travelled slowly, and the wandering pedlar was as welcome for his news as for his wares. Now, from newspapers, wireless, and television we learn the latest news from all over the world.

The Countryside and the Town

To modern eyes, Scotland in the sixteenth century would seem a poor country. But writers who lived then were impressed by the prosperous appearance of both the countryside and the towns. The Lothians, for example, were—then as now—extremely fertile, while Clydesdale with its rich harvests of corn and beasts and coal was described as 'the paradise of Scotland'. Fife, fortunate in its fertile soil, its coal and salt workings, and its busy little seaports, was 'a grey cloth mantle with a golden fringe'.

Among the towns, Dundee was considered 'one of the finest towns in Scotland', Aberdeen 'a rich and handsome

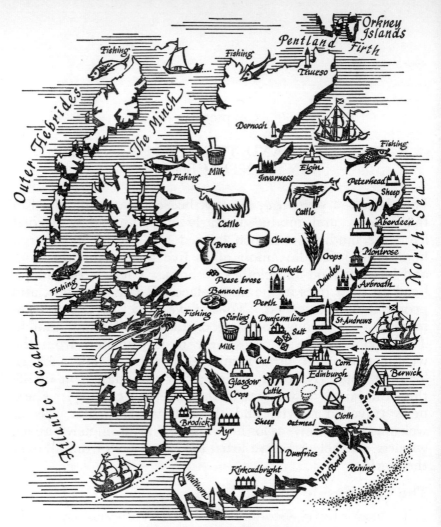

16TH CENTURY SCOTLAND
Main Towns and Fertile Areas

town inhabited by an excellent people', Perth 'a very pretty place', and Montrose 'a beautiful town with a very good harbour'. Edinburgh, the capital, was praised for its High Street, which was as wide as a market place. Of Glasgow, then an open town round the cathedral, one visitor wrote, 'This flourishing city reminds me of the beautiful fabrics and the florid fields of England'.

Besides being represented in Parliament, the royal burghs sent members to their own assembly, the Convention of Royal Burghs. By a law of 1578, they were allowed to meet four times a year, in any burgh they chose. If your town is a royal burgh, it would have been represented there. The members talked about trade, ships, customs duties, and the affairs of the Scottish trading post at Campvere in the Netherlands. When Parliament levied taxes, the Convention decided how much each town was to pay. The Convention still meets, and includes members from Paisley, Airdrie, and Greenock, which, though not royal burghs, are now places of importance.

The People

What of the people who lived in Scotland four hundred years ago? Most of them have left no records, and we know little about them. Country folk lived as their forefathers had done, keeping flocks, cultivating the infield and avoiding the marshy lowlands. In normal years, they produced enough to keep themselves alive. They had plenty of sheep and cattle, and fish were abundant, but because of their primitive farming methods and wet summers, grain crops were sometimes poor. In years of famine, some people starved: in years of plenty, some corn was exported.

The Highlanders lived on meat, milk, and cheese from their herds, and fish from the rivers. In the Lowlands bread was more common. Oatmeal made the porridge, the brose, the bannocks, and the oatcakes eaten by most of the people. Pease-meal, a flour made from ground peas, was the food of the poorest.

Men had to work hard with plough and sickle and flail, with axe and peatspade, and the women were always busy grinding corn, or baking on the girdle, or making the family clothes.

In the Borders, riding into Northumberland and driving off English cattle was so common that it might almost be called an industry. Walter Scott of Harden—'Auld Wat' as he was called—was the most famous of these Border reivers.

E

When stocks of meat were running low, his wife Mary would lay before him at dinner-time an ashet with nothing on it but a pair of spurs. This was the sign for him to lead his men over the Cheviots again.

> The dark has heard them gather,
>   The dawn has bowed them by,
> To the guard on the roof comes the drum of a hoof
>   And the drone of a hoof's reply.
> There are more than birds on the hill to-night,
>   And more than winds on the plain!
> The threat of the Scotts has filled the moss,
>   'There will be moonlight again'.[1]

Of course, the English made similar raids, as you may read in the ballad, *Jamie Telfer in the Fair Dodhead*.

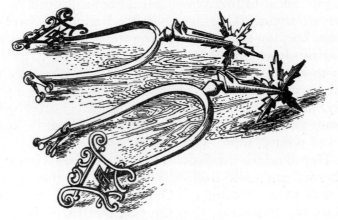

THE HARDEN SPURS

Dress

Scottish merchants who traded abroad were ordered to dress well, so that foreigners would be impressed. The Scotsman abroad might not always be wealthy, but he put on a bold face to the world: he was proud of himself and his finery. Laws of a different kind were required at home.

[1] From *Ho! For The Blades of Harden*, by Will H. Ogilvie.

The ordinary man in the burghs could be recognised by his 'blue bonnet and plaid', but most people seem to have been guilty of dressing too well.   In 1581, families with land worth less than 2000 merks a year were banned from wearing cloth of gold or silver, velvet or satin, or even imported woollen cloth.   In those days, a man's clothes were a clue to his rank.   In 1575, ministers and their wives were ordered not to wear bright colours, embroidered clothes, or jewellery. All their clothes were to be of dark colours, such as 'black, russet, sad grey, sad brown'.   From this law, 'clerical grey' was born.

The Parson of Stobo

Before the Reformation, clergymen were not in the habit of wearing dark clothes, as we shall learn when we meet Adam Colquhoun, the parson of Stobo.   He lives in his manse in Glasgow, but draws a yearly income of two thousand pounds Scots from two parishes in the upper Tweed valley, which he visits sometimes to supervise the vicar whom he pays to take his place.

As he stands at the manse door to greet us, we are struck by the brightness of his clothes: the scarlet of his doublet and waistcoat, the whiteness of his shirt, the gold trimmings on his belt and his velvet cap.   Over his arm he carries a fine gown with a fur collar.   He likes velvet, the dearest of cloths, and marten, the choicest of furs.

His house is a great stone tower.   It is dark as we stumble up the spiral staircase.   In the hall, we admire the fine tapestries which cover the stone walls.   Then we gaze at the fire, a fire of 'black stones' (coal) burning in an iron grate. In this room the parson eats at his meat-board, a table-top resting on trestles.   He opens the doors of his carved cupboard to display his treasures—forty silver plates and vessels, two dozen silver spoons, a dozen small knives and a fork. We are surprised to see the knives and the fork, because men usually carry their own knives or use their daggers for cutting meat.   People usually lift meat with their fingers instead of using forks.

In the Parson of Stobo's Hall

He is well supplied with 'belly cheer'. In his barn he has wheat, barley and oats, and in his cellar eight salted carcasses of beef, eight dozen salmon, six stones of butter, as well as plenty of cheeses, oatmeal, and herring.

He is proud of his bedroom. He sleeps in a fine, carved bed, on a soft mattress thick with feathers, with fine sheets, two plaids, and two blankets to keep him warm. Curtains hang round the bed to keep out the draught. There is so much to amaze the ordinary man of Colquhoun's time—a bed which is a piece of furniture, walls whose stonework is hidden behind the tapestry hangings, the oak settle by the fireplace, the wardrobe for keeping clothes in, and all the chests full of valuables. Suddenly there is a squawk and we shriek in terror. It's a bird—a bird of many colours with a hooked beak! The parson talks to it and tells us that it is his pet—a parrot.

Merchants

As long as Scotland and England were enemies, little trade took place between them. It was to Europe, and especially to the Netherlands, that Scottish merchants shipped their exports. To the skilful Flemish weavers went raw wool, by far the most valuable cargo. The king's officers at the ports collected one pound in customs duty after 1346 on every sack of wool. Leith, Aberdeen, and Dundee controlled most of this trade. The ports of the north-east sent out salted salmon, while Leith, Crail, Dumbarton, Ayr, and Irvine handled the herring trade. Everything sold abroad by Scottish merchants came from either farming or fishing.

One Scottish merchant, Andrew Halliburton, kept a detailed account of everything he bought and sold. Bishops, dukes, and merchants were his customers. He states in a letter in 1502 that he sold one sack of wool for twenty-two merks, and another sack for twenty-three merks, and adds, 'Hides, I think, shall be the best merchandise to come here at Easter for there are many folk that ask about them'. The goods he brought back in his ship were a mixed cargo—lengths of coloured cloth, books, hats, floor-tiles, wine, spices, thread for embroidery, church vessels, and a tombstone.

We may say generally that Scotland gave large quantities of a few simple products in return for smaller amounts of a wide range of luxury goods.

Later in the sixteenth century, when the abbeys decayed, the burghs became more important. The merchants, bound together in their merchant gilds, gradually gained control of their burghs by becoming town councillors. In this way, the men who traded secured power over the men who made things—the craftsmen.

Francis Spottiswood, the cloth merchant, works in a booth below his house in Edinburgh. He is wearing a brown coat and red stockings, but what catches our eye is his purse with gold tassels hanging from his belt. Truly a man of money! He picks a bale of woollen cloth from the nearest chest, and unrolls it on the counter for us to inspect it. When he takes us to see his house, we go out into the street and climb the forestairs. We enter the hall or main room, where we see the table and cupboard like the parson of Stobo's, but Francis Spottiswood has been spending his money on luxuries—a tablecloth, a silver salt-cellar, and a chair for himself at the head of the table. Over there in the corner is his suit of armour, his helmet, and his two-handed sword, for he must always be ready to help defend the town.

IN THE MERCHANT'S HALL

The bedroom is not only a place to sleep in. The 'muckle wheel' at the far end of the room is being used by Mrs. Spottiswood for spinning. An important invention, the 'muckle wheel' can spin yarn simply by turning the wheel. Mrs. Spottiswood tells us how pleased she is that the old, laborious way of spinning with spindle and whorl is dying

SPINNING WITH THE 'MUCKLE WHEEL'

out, and that most homes now have a 'muckle wheel'. She spins quite quickly, but she has to wind the yarn by hand. What is over there? You can see yourself in it. Mrs Spottiswood calls it a 'keiking glass.'

Francis Spottiswood, the cloth merchant, owns a horse, a plough, a pair of harrows, a cart, and a sledge. Like other burgesses, he has a share in 'the burgh acres', from which most of his food comes.

Schoolboys

Most boys and girls did not attend school at all. As soon as they were old enough they helped in the fields or in the house. In the burghs, boys became apprentices until they learned a trade. For boys who did attend school, the hours were long. At Aberdeen Grammar School, scholars had spent two hours in class by nine o'clock in the morning. After an hour's break, they were back at their lessons until twelve o'clock, and in the afternoon they were at work from two until four and again from five o'clock until six. James Melville, who went to school in Montrose, tells how he and his fellows studied the Bible, Latin, and French, and 'be our maister war teached to handle the bow for archerie, the glub for goff, the batons for fencing, also to rin, to loope, to swoom, to warsell'.

Something for You to Do

1. The population of Scotland has increased considerably since 1557, but some places have increased in size more than others. Here are the chief Scottish burghs in order of importance in 1557 and 1957.

1557 (Based on taxable value)	1957 (Based on population)
Edinburgh	Glasgow
Dundee	Edinburgh
Aberdeen	Aberdeen
Perth	Dundee
St. Andrews	Paisley
Montrose	Greenock
Cupar	Motherwell and
Ayr	Wishaw
Glasgow	Kirkcaldy
Dunfermline	Coatbridge
Dumfries	Clydebank
Inverness	Dunfermline
Stirling	Kilmarnock
	Ayr

(a) Is your town here? Has it risen or declined in importance compared with the other burghs in Scotland?

(b) Make a list of the burghs which have risen most.

(c) Why do you think they have risen?

2. Explain the following: the Convention of Royal Burghs; Border reivers; 'sad grey'; 'belly cheer'; forestairs; 'muckle wheel'; 'keiking glass'.

3. Make a list of the luxuries which the parson and merchant owned but which most people in the sixteenth century did not have.

4. Make a list of the contents of a modern council house which make it more comfortable and easier to manage than a laird's tower four hundred years ago.

5. Compare Scotland's imports and exports in the sixteenth century.

6. Rewrite in English what James Melville was taught at school.

Chapter 22

THE STRUGGLE FOR FREEDOM

1. *The Reign of James VI and I*

The Union of the Crowns

In the lives of most Scottish people, the year 1603 brought no change. In 1603, however, Queen Elizabeth, the last of the Tudors, died, having named James VI of Scotland to succeed her. To James the news came like the fulfilment of a dream. England was a powerful nation, whose sailors like Sir Francis Drake had faced the naval might of Spain and scattered or sunk the proud Armada only fifteen years before. It was a far richer country, where agriculture and trade prospered. There, the Renaissance flowered in the plays of William Shakespeare. Besides, England had a Church after his own heart—a Church with bishops in control. 'Jamie Saxt', King of Scotland, became James I, King of England, without a blow struck in anger. Little wonder that he felt God was on his side!

James and his courtiers departed for London, the capital of his greater kingdom. He was not sorry to leave Scotland. For years the nobles had struggled to control him, and the ministers of the Kirk had thundered their independence

from the pulpits. He was to return to his native land only
once in the next twenty-two years. Only the merchants of
Edinburgh were sorry to see him go. Their trade suffered,
as not only the king but many of his nobles departed, to
buy their wines, cloth, and other luxuries in London.

Although Great Britain was now subject to one king,
Scotland and England remained separate in other ways.
They kept their own systems of law. Their Churches were
different: the Church of England was Episcopalian, that is,
under the control of bishops, but in Scotland the Kirk was
Presbyterian, with freedom to run its own affairs. The
bishops whom James had appointed in Scotland were
members of Parliament, but at first they had no authority
in the Kirk. Each country retained its own parliament.
James hoped for a closer union between the two nations,
because he could see that sooner or later the interests of the
two countries were bound to clash, but his proposals were
rejected by the English parliament.

James in England

James found the English parliament a dangerous rival to
his own power. Parliament maintained that the king could
not make laws or levy taxes within the country without its
consent. If the king did not recognise its rights it could cut
his supply of money. Parliament was liable to push its
claims further against a foreign king like James than it had
dared to do against Queen Elizabeth.

In James's time, no one considered that all men should be
free to worship as they pleased. No one would then have
imagined that we should have many different Churches
to-day, or that people would now be able to attend any
Church they liked. To-day, we have *religious toleration*, but
in the seventeenth century each religious group believed
that it alone worshipped in the right way, and tried to
convert all the others to share its beliefs and services.

Many English people were *Puritans*. They lived strict
lives, they liked to read the Bible, and wanted to worship
in a simple manner. When James met some of them at

Hampton Court in 1604, they had high hopes that he, coming from Presbyterian Scotland, would make some of the changes that they wished to see in the Church of England. But when they mentioned Presbytery, where, as the king said, 'Tom and Will and Dick may meet and censure me', he was reminded of his struggles with the Kirk in Scotland. He dismissed them without letting them have their own way, but he did agree to a new translation of the Bible being made. This, the *Authorised Version* as it is known, is the translation commonly used by Protestants to-day. It is addressed to 'the Most High and Mighty Prince, James, by the Grace of God, King of Great Britain, France and Ireland, Defender of the Faith'.

In 1620, some Puritans known as 'Pilgrim Fathers' set sail from Plymouth in the ship *Mayflower*, braving the wild Atlantic to seek freedom on the North American shore.

Even Roman Catholics were disappointed by this son of a Catholic queen. The plot by some Catholics to blow up the king and Parliament with gunpowder was betrayed, and Guy Fawkes was arrested in a cellar on the 4th November 1605. Nowadays, the opening of Parliament by the queen is preceded by a ceremonial inspection of the cellars by the Yeomen of the Guard. The Fifth of November, the intended date of the explosion, is still 'Guy Fawkes Night' throughout the country.

James and Scotland

Because he controlled the Privy Council, James was able to rule Scotland according to his wishes. He was sure that the Scottish Parliament would not oppose him, because 'his men' were certain of being elected to the *Committee of the Articles*, which drew up the 'articles' or bills that pleased the king. The full Parliament met simply to approve them. James spoke the truth when he declared: 'This I must say for Scotland and may truly vaunt [boast] it. Here I sit and govern it with my pen. I write and it is done, and by a Clerk of the Council I govern Scotland now, which others could not do by the sword'.

Quietly and purposefully, he laboured to bring the Church of Scotland under his control. The General Assembly, for long the voice of the Scottish ministers and people, was not allowed to meet without his permission. The bishops he had appointed in Scotland were given real power. James felt that he had won the struggle and was master over the Kirk. His next step was to change the form of service in the churches and to make it the same as that followed by the Church of England. For example, he ordered people to kneel when they were taking Communion. But it was one thing to make changes: it was more difficult to have them obeyed, as Charles I, James's son, was to discover.

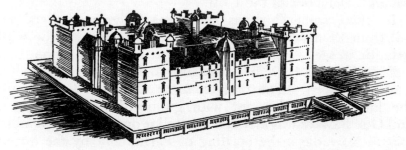

GEORGE HERIOT'S SCHOOL, EDINBURGH
Completed about 1650

Something for You to Do

1. Why was James VI anxious to become king of England?
2. Find out more about some of the men who made England famous in the Elizabethan age.
3. (a) Which party in the church in England did James favour, and why?
   (b) What other religious groups did James find in England, and how did he deal with them?
4. How did James make sure that his orders were carried out in Scotland?
5. Make a time-chart of *Britain in Stewart Times* (1603-1714), using a suitable scale, with columns for *Date, Ruler, Events in Scotland*, and *Events in England*. Put in important events from this and later chapters.

Chapter 23

THE STRUGGLE FOR FREEDOM

2. *Charles I and Cromwell*

When Charles I succeeded his father in 1625, he was the first king of Scotland to be more English than Scottish. He ruled as a foreigner, and he ruled from a distance as his father had done, but he showed no understanding of the Scots or of the Church of Scotland. In England, Parliament struggled to limit his power, but in Scotland, where Parliament carried out his bidding, it was the Kirk that he had most to fear.

Soon he made other enemies in Scotland. Many of the Scottish nobles had seized lands from the Church during the Reformation. These lands had been in their families' hands for over sixty years, and had come to be regarded as their own. But in 1625 Charles ordered all landowners who held Church lands to restore them to the Crown, and so drove the nobles into a firm alliance with the Kirk.

Charles ordered a new Scottish prayer book, similar to that used in the Church of England, to be read in all the Scottish churches. Its first reading in St. Giles' in Edinburgh was met by a shower of stools and stones hurled by the indignant congregation. This was the beginning of active opposition by the Presbyterians.

In 1638, the *National Covenant* was drawn up and signed in Greyfriars' Kirk in Edinburgh. All over the southern half of the country, people eagerly put their names to copies. Those who signed, now called *Covenanters*, promised to maintain 'the true religion'—that is, the practices of the Church of Scotland—and also to defend the king. You may think that it would be impossible for the Covenanters to carry out both these promises, since the king appeared to

141

THE SPIRE, KIRK OF ST. GILES

be attacking the Church of Scotland. Most people then believed that William Laud, the Archbishop of Canterbury, was responsible for the Prayer Book, and that Charles was under his influence. The time came when those who signed the Covenant had to decide which was their greater loyalty —to their king or to their Church. Most of them chose to fight for the Kirk; some, led by the Marquis of Montrose, preferred to do their duty to the king.

Thus the Scots challenged the king. They were about to embark on a war of religion, similar to the *Thirty Years' War* (1618-48) which was then being waged on the Continent. Many of their leaders were battle-hardened veterans of that war. They had served as 'soldiers of fortune' in the armies of Gustavus Adolphus, the Protestant king of Sweden. Their commander was the 'old, little, crooked soldier', Alexander Leslie, who had risen to command the Swedish forces in Germany after the death of Gustavus. The Covenanters formed a strong, dedicated army. Most of their 20,000 soldiers were 'stout young plewmen. . . . Had ye lent your eare in the morning, or especialle at even, and heard in the tents the sound of some singing psalms, some praying and some reading scripture, you would have been refreshed.'

Their advance into England found Charles without an army strong enough to stop them, and he had to allow them to have their own Kirk again. He had lost control of Scotland completely.

THE FLAG OF THE COVENANTERS

The Covenanters and the Civil War

Early in his reign, Charles had quarrelled with the English Parliament, and for the next eleven years (1629-40) he had been ruling without it. Now, needing extra money to pay and supply an army, he had no option but to summon Parliament again. Parliament wanted to reduce his power, and to make sure that he did not rule on his own again. The two sides could not agree, and the *Civil War* broke out.

Charles's followers, the *Cavaliers*, came from the ranks of the country landowners and their men, while Parliament's army, nicknamed *Roundheads*, consisted mainly of craftsmen and merchants from the towns, and prosperous farmers like

Oliver Cromwell.   Charles 1.   Marquis of Montrose.

Oliver Cromwell. Most of the Roundheads were Puritans, and some were Presbyterians like the Scots. The two sides were well-matched: the support of the Scottish army could be decisive. The Covenanters agreed to fight on Parliament's side, on condition that religion was established in England 'according to the word of God and the example of the best reformed Churches'. To the Scots, that meant Presbyterianism. While fighting against a king who forced his religion on them, the Scots were at the same time trying to force a Church like their own on the English people. In 1644, at *Marston Moor* in Yorkshire, Leslie's foot-soldiers helped Oliver Cromwell's magnificent cavalry—the *Ironsides*—to overwhelm the Cavaliers.

A Cavalier

Meanwhile, the Marquis of Montrose, one of those who had signed the National Covenant, could not set aside his oath to defend the king, and raised forces to fight for him in Scotland. With a small army of Irishmen and Highlanders, he swept through Scotland like a whirlwind. Thanks to his speed of movement and his own brilliant leadership, he won six victories in a single year—between September 1644 and August 1645. Scotland was in his hand. He would now invade England to help King Charles. But his forces were surprised at *Philiphaugh* near Selkirk by David Leslie's army of Covenanters. The battle became a rout, and the rout a massacre, in revenge for the slaughter of the people of Aberdeen by Montrose's men a year before.

Successes at Philiphaugh in Scotland and at *Naseby* in England made 1645 a year of victory for Cromwell's army and the Covenanters. Four years later Charles I, now the prisoner of the Parliamentary army, was tried by Parliament and put to death on the scaffold. Horror spread among the Scottish people. They had wanted victory for their religion, but not at the expense of the life of their king. His son, Charles II, was immediately proclaimed king of Scotland, but in England a republic known as the *Commonwealth* was established.

A Puritan

Cromwell and Scotland

Charles's presence in Scotland drew Cromwell's army northwards. At *Dunbar*, the Covenanters and Roundheads, formerly comrades-in-arms at Marston Moor, came face to face in battle. The Covenanters were placed in a strong position by David Leslie, but the ministers in his camp persuaded him to move his army down the hill. This was just what Cromwell wanted. 'The Lord has delivered them into our hands,' he said, as he sent his Ironsides crashing through the Scottish lines. Exactly a year later, on the 3rd September 1651, he crushed a Scottish invasion of England at the battle of *Worcester*.

An army of occupation under General Monk prevented further rebellion in Scotland. Even in the Highlands, law and order were maintained as never before. As an Englishman observed, 'A man may ride all over Scotland with a switch in his hand and a hundred pounds in his pocket, which he could not have done these five hundred years.' Religious toleration was granted to all. Scotland had the right to send representatives to the British Parliament in London, but the Scots were well aware that this union of Scotland and England was maintained by the force of Cromwell's armies, and that they themselves had to pay the bill.

Something for You to Do

1. What mistakes did Charles I make in dealing with the Scots?
2. Write notes on: the Scottish Prayer Book; the National Covenant; Cavaliers; Roundheads; the Commonwealth.
3. What were the parts played in the Civil War by (a) the Marquis of Montrose; (b) Alexander Leslie; (c) David Leslie?
4. How did Scotland (a) *benefit*, and (b) *suffer*, under Cromwell?
5. Continue your time chart.

Chapter 24

THE STRUGGLE FOR FREEDOM

3. *From Restoration to Revolution*

Cromwell's government was effective but unpopular, and when he died there was no strong man to succeed him. General Monk, the commander of the Commonwealth forces in Scotland, was convinced that only the return of the king would satisfy the people. He marched his army south to London, and recalled Charles II from exile. Britain's only experiment with republican government came to an end.

The *Restoration*, as the return of the king was called, took place in 1660. It was an occasion for revelry and rejoicing, the noise of trumpets, bells, and cannon, bonfires, drinking, and dancing in the streets. The king was back, and Scotland was independent once more. But soon the people ceased to rejoice.

Charles controlled Scotland, as his grandfather had done, 'with the pen'. Bishops were again appointed to rule the Church, and the National Covenant was declared illegal. The right to choose ministers was taken from congregations and given to local landowners. As a result, nearly three hundred ministers, mainly in the south-west of Scotland, gave up their churches and their incomes, and led their congregations to worship outside in *conventicles* among the hills.

Among them were John Blackadder, who preached to an assembly of four thousand people near Cramond, John Welsh the great-grandson of John Knox, Alexander Peden who for twenty years lived and preached in the open air, and Richard Cameron, an outspoken crusader for Christ. These

146

'outed' ministers preached under the threat of sentence of death, and, risking fines and horrible torture by the 'boot' and thumbscrews, the people came to hear them. Ministers and people were persecuted, but they took courage from the word of God: 'Blessed are they which are persecuted for righteousness' sake: for theirs is the kingdom of heaven'.

A Conventicle

See them setting off from the distant village, some walking, some riding, the men carrying weapons, till they reach the appointed hollow in the hills. Sentries are posted to look out in all directions for the hated red-coats. The women pull heather to sit on. 'There now, see that man in black, pulling off his mask. That's the minister—that's Sandy Peden.' He leads them in worship, talking to them in homely, simple terms. 'I will tell you where the Church is,' he says—'It is wherever a praying young man or young woman is, at a dykeside in Scotland. That is where the Church is.' The service is not interrupted to-day by the shout of the sentry or the warning cry of the peewit, and at its close the people return quietly to their homes. The wandering Peden goes with them, to share a meal but not to sleep, for he spends his nights under the stars.

The Covenanters Fight

The laws against conventicles drove the Covenanters into rebellion. From Galloway and Ayrshire, they marched towards Edinburgh—a brave little army, some armed only with scythes and pitchforks. In 1666, at *Rullion Green* in the Pentlands, they were overwhelmed by royalist forces under Dalyell of the Binns, who had learned his soldiering in Russia. Torture and hanging were the lot of those taken prisoner. In a 'reign of terror', soldiers under Dalyell and Graham of Claverhouse scoured the country in search of Covenanters.

In 1679, a handful of Covenanters dragged Archbishop Sharp from his coach on Magus Muir near St. Andrews and killed him before his daughter's eyes. Sharp had been a

Presbyterian minister, but had deserted to the king's side to become a bishop and the persecutor of his former friends. Both sides carried on the fight with desperate fury, until a large government army broke the back of the rebellion at the battle of *Bothwell Bridge*. A thousand Covenanters were taken prisoner and marched to Edinburgh, where most were pardoned on condition that they would not rebel again, but over two hundred of them were transported to the colonies.

Extremists, called *Cameronians* after their leader Richard Cameron, were hunted and put to death. In Wigtownshire the 'two Margarets', Margaret Wilson, a girl of eighteen, and Margaret MacLachlan, were tied to stakes and drowned by the incoming Solway tide. Those who perished during this 'killing time' for what they believed to be the truth are the subject of Robert Louis Stevenson's famous poem:

> Blows the wind to-day, and the sun and the rain are flying,
>   Blows the wind on the moors to-day and now,
> Where about the graves of the martyrs the whaups are crying,
>   My heart remembers how!
>
> Grey recumbent tombs of the dead in desert places,
>   Standing-stones on the vacant wine-red moor,
> Hills of sheep, and the homes of the silent vanquished races,
>   And winds austere and pure.
>
> Be it granted me to behold you again in dying,
>   Hills of home! And to hear again the call;
> Hear about the graves of the martyrs the peewees crying,
>   And hear no more at all.

'The Glorious Revolution'

The next king, James VII and II, was a Roman Catholic. In 1687 he issued the first of two *Declarations of Indulgence*, which allowed Presbyterians and Roman Catholics, as well as members of the Church of England, to worship freely. It was a sensible end to a generation of persecution, but James's motives were suspected because he was a Roman Catholic.

In England, he appointed Roman Catholics to high positions in the State and in the Army, although this was against the law. When his son was born in 1688, people dreaded the prospect of years of rule by Catholic monarchs in what was mainly a Protestant country. William of Orange, James's son-in-law, was asked to come over from Holland to preserve Protestantism in Britain.

William came, and James fled. William, and his wife Mary, became king and queen of England by accepting the conditions laid down in the *Bill of Rights* in 1689. Since that time a monarch has had to be Protestant, and his authority has been limited. For raising taxes, having an army in peace time, altering old laws or passing new ones, he has had to rely on Parliament. He has had no power to do any of these things without Parliament's consent. As a result, Parliament became a partner the king could not do without in governing the country. This great change, which took place peacefully in England, was known as 'The Glorious, Bloodless Revolution'.

We Promise

1. Not to be a Roman Catholic

2. Not to tax without the consent of Parliament

3. Not to raise a standing army in peace-time without the consent of Parliament

4. Not to alter the Laws

Signed William Mary

THE BILL OF RIGHTS
The Four Promises

In Scotland also, William and Mary became joint rulers. When the Committee of the Articles was abolished in 1690, Scotland secured a Parliament which was free for the first time to propose and debate new laws. In the Highlands, however, Graham of Claverhouse (now Viscount Dundee) raised the clans in James's favour. He defeated the government troops at the battle of *Killiecrankie* (1689), but when he was himself killed the rebellion petered out.

Scotland became Presbyterian in religion. The bishops were deposed, and Andrew Melville's ideal of a Presbyterian Church independent of royal control was triumphant. The General Assembly met in 1690, for the first time since the days of Cromwell, and has met every year since, as the voice of the nation's Kirk. The Kirk had won its struggle against the king. Religious toleration was granted to members of other Protestant Churches, and people began to accept this newer and broader ideal of freedom for everyone to worship as he pleased.

Something for You to Do

1. Was there a Covenanting minister in your district? If so, find out all you can about him, and the places where conventicles were held.
2. Write notes on: Dalyell of the Binns; Graham of Claverhouse; the Wigtownshire Martyrs; Declarations of Indulgence.
3. In what ways did the Bill of Rights limit the monarch's power in England?
4. What benefits did the 'Glorious Revolution' bring to Scotland?
5. Continue your time chart.
6. Two interesting novels about the Covenanters are *I Rode with the Covenanters*, by Kathleen Fidler, and *Bonfire in the Wind*, by Jane Oliver.

Chapter 25

LIFE IN THE HIGHLANDS IN THE SEVENTEENTH CENTURY

While the population of Scotland has steadily increased in the last two hundred years, the proportion living in the Highlands has gradually diminished. We shall see the reasons for the drift of people from the Highlands in Book Two. Nowadays, every summer sees the return of people with Highland names from Glasgow, Edinburgh, and other Scottish industrial towns, from England, from the U.S.A., and from Commonwealth countries like Canada, Australia, and New Zealand, to visit the glens of their ancestors.

Let us take a look at the old way of life of the Highlanders, as it was in the seventeenth century.

The *Highland Line*, which separates Highlanders from Lowlanders, runs along the edge of the Highlands where they drop down to the Lowlands, roughly twenty miles north of Glasgow, Stirling, Perth, and Montrose. It continues northwards and westwards, leaving out most of Aberdeenshire and the flatter lands along the Moray Firth. The Highlanders occupy the lands north and west of the Highland Line.

The Highlanders were still organised in clans, each under its own chief. The word *clan* means 'the children', and suggests that the members of one clan were all related to one another. Certainly, the chief was in the position of an all-powerful father over them. They paid rents and labour services to him. He was their judge, and his word was law. He was their commander, who would call them to follow him when the 'fiery cross', charred in fire and smeared with blood, was sent round to summon the clan to war. The most important members of the clan, called *tacksmen*, were related to the chief and held their land directly from him, usually in return for low rents. They had the clan surname, but all the other clansmen were in the clan because they were on the chief's land. Thus, Macintyres were members of the Clan Campbell.

The chief held the land of the clan. He kept some, called *mensal land*, for himself, he gave pieces to personal attendants

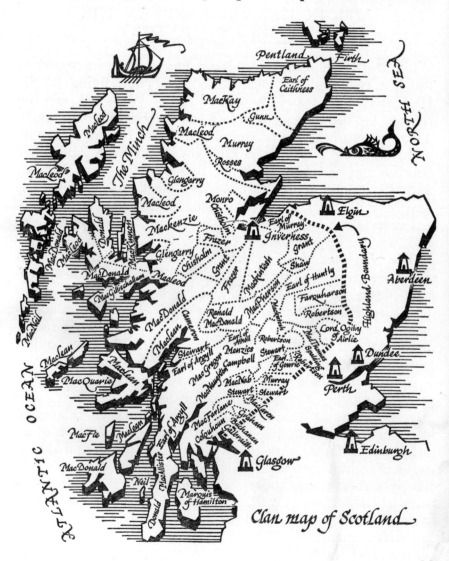

Clan map of Scotland

like the bard, the harper, and the piper, and split the rest on *tack*, or lease, to his relatives. They in turn let their land to sub-tenants, who paid for it by working the tacksmen's land and looking after their cattle. By this arrangement, the tacksmen were sure of a living without having to work. They were the privileged members of the clan and the chief fighting men.

The poorer clansmen were in a less happy position. In the Western Isles before 1600 it is recorded that 'na labourers of the ground are permitted to steir furth of the cuntrie quhatevir their masters have ado, except only gentlemen quhilk labouris not, that the labour belonging to the teiling of the ground and the wynning of thair corns may not be left undone'. The people had to herd their cattle and sheep constantly to protect them from raiders and wild animals like foxes and wolves.[1] The 'black cattle', which might also be reddish or dark-brown in colour, were the Highlanders' main source of wealth. In May the herds drove them to the hill pastures for the summer. The women lived up there in the shielings and made butter and cheese. In September many of the beasts were taken by drovers to be sold at the Cattle Tryst at Crieff, because there was not enough feeding to keep them all through the winter. Highland cows gave a small supply of milk, only a Scots pint [2] a day, compared with four gallons from a good Ayrshire cow at the present time. Sheep, too, were milked, besides providing a wool that was fine but small in quantity. Little wool was exported, but it was used to clothe the Highlanders.

Arable land was scarce, and often consisted of small patches only. In some places it was cultivated with a wooden plough pulled by four highland ponies, and in the more inaccessible uplands with a *caschrom*. The crop of oats was used for making oatcakes and porridge, but the Highlanders, who never grew enough corn for themselves, made up their supplies by bartering their cattle with the Lowland farmers for grain.

[1] The last wolf was killed in 1743.
[2] Equal to three English pints.

Clans nearest to the Lowlands stole cattle and drove them home. Sometimes they levied blackmail and, in return for a sum of money, promised to protect a farmer's cattle. Raiding was a common occupation for the Highlander, as a letter written by Cameron of Lochiel shows. His men had been accused of raiding a farm belonging to one of the Grants, but Lochiel protested—'My men were not in your bounds but in Murray [Moray] lands where all men take their prey.'

Clan feuds, cattle-reiving, and droving all required the Highlander to be a skilled fighter. His chief weapon was a basket-hilted broadsword. It left him one hand free, and he carried on his left arm a targe and in his left hand a dirk. His round targe, covered with studded leather, had a long spike in the centre, and was useful in attack as well as defence. Thus armed, Highlanders in war always sought high ground from which to charge down on their enemies.

A man's main garment was the *plaid* or 'great wrap', wrapped round his waist and not reaching his knees, the remainder being thrown over his shoulder or else covering the upper part of his body as a cloak. His plaid served him as a blanket as well. It could be a hindrance in war, and before an attack the Highlanders took off their plaids and charged in their shirts. Women wore self-coloured dresses of wool and linen, and a checked plaid over their shoulders. At this time, no clan had a distinctive tartan, and clansmen were distinguished in battle by the emblems they wore in their bonnets. The MacDonalds of Clanranald, for example, wore heather, and the Frasers sprigs of yew.

The Highlander lived in a simple house, with a thatched roof, and thick walls of uncemented stones. Since he spent most of his life out of doors, he regarded his house as a shelter from the rain, the wind, and the cold, a shelter for both man and beast. His cow was valuable to him, and occupied the byre at one end of the house. The door, the only outside door, opened into the byre, and to reach the living quarters he passed through a lobby between two box-beds into the kitchen. There a peat-fire burned, warming the cooking-pot which was suspended by a chain from the rafters. Only a wooden partition separated 'the little room' from the kitchen.

Box-beds with heather to lie on, a few three-legged stools and a bench to sit on—these were usually the only articles of furniture. The women spun with spindle and whorl by the glint of the fire. The family sat 'round the fire' on stools or flat stones, and near the partition door there was usually a stone for any wanderer who might want to come in.

THE HIGHLANDER'S HOUSE

The people lived in hamlets, for there were few towns. Until 1641 most of the trade of the north and west was in the hands of the merchants of Inverness. Gradually, markets and fairs were started in new burghs like Wick and Dingwall, or in places like Portree, where two fairs were held each year after 1693. Highland women might want ribbons, spoons, wooden plates, combs, and shears, but they had little to sell in return—a cheese or two, a little butter, or some woollen cloth. For most of them, the wandering chapman or pedlar supplied what they needed and could afford from the outside world.

It was difficult to make the Highlanders as law-abiding as the people in the south. After the MacGregors had massacred many of the Clan Colquhoun, James VI gave orders in 1603 'for the utter extermination of all that race'. The MacGregors were outlawed, losing their lands and even their names. Many took refuge by adopting new names in other clans. The *Statutes of Iona* (1609), drawn up by the Bishop of Iona and the western chiefs, helped to cut down private wars and to make most of the clans in these parts faithful to the Episcopal Church. Roman Catholicism kept its hold over clans like the MacDonalds. It gained strength from the work of Franciscan preachers who, like St. Columba, came over from Ireland. These two Churches, Episcopal and Catholic, made the Highlanders, with the notable exception of the Campbells, staunch opponents of the Presbyterian Church which the Covenanters were fighting to establish.

Something for You to Do

1. (a) If you have a Highland name, find out the clan to which you belong, its district, tartan, and emblem. See *The Scottish Clans and their Tartans* (Johnston & Bacon).

   (b) If you are at school outside the Highlands, count the number of pupils with Highland names in your class, and you will have some idea of the amount of Highland migration to your district.

2. Write notes on: clan; fiery cross; tacksman; mensal land; shieling; blackmail; broadsword; plaid; chapman.

3. Why did the Covenanters gain little support in the Highlands?

4. Either draw a plan of a Highlander's house, or make a model with plasticine. Push stone chips into the plasticine walls to give a 'dry-stone' effect. Use match-boxes for box-beds and for the partition. The roof, which should be detachable to show the ground-plan, can be made of plasticine or foam-rubber.

Chapter 26

LIFE IN THE BURGHS IN THE
SEVENTEENTH CENTURY

Although most people still lived and worked in the country, the burghs were important places where goods were made and trade went on. The earliest burghs were the royal burghs, which claimed that the right to hold markets and fairs belonged to them alone. Their privileges were seriously challenged during the seventeenth century, for no fewer than 125 new burghs of barony were created. In many cases, the main village on the lord's land was given the right to hold a market. If it was a good centre, it might sometimes win trade from a nearby royal burgh.

There were many burghs in Fife. As Sir Walter Scott's character Andrew Fairservice said, 'There's the Kingdom of Fife, frae Culross to the East Neuk, it's just like a great combined city—sae mony royal burghs yoked end on end.' These ports faced the Forth, and their ships plied their trade with Europe across the North Sea.

One of them, Culross,[1] used to be a village sheltering outside an abbey wall. Early in the seventeenth century, it was a royal burgh and a flourishing port. The Civil War, and the wars between the English and Dutch, interrupted Scotland's trade with Holland so much that Fletcher of Saltoun was driven to declare at the end of the century that 'the Fife seaports once very prosperous are in our day little better than so many heaps of ruins.' Culross fell asleep until the present century, when the restoration of its old buildings by the National Trust for Scotland has preserved a seventeenth-century burgh for us to see to-day.

[1] Pronounced *Cooris*.

CULROSS

The Thriving Burgh of Culross

If you visit it now it is not difficult to imagine it as it was.
You have stepped back in time; you are in a seventeenth-
century burgh. Walk along the narrow streets and you
will see that they are *causewayed*, that is, paved with flat
stones high in the centre or 'croon'. There are no pavements.
The merchants walk on the 'croon', and apprentices or
children have to stay on the side till they pass. The houses
are built of stone, with low doorways and little windows.
Some houses have harled walls painted in pleasant colours.
Many of the gable-ends are *crow-stepped* or 'corbie-stoned'.
The Scottish mason is a practical man who has special reasons
for building like this. The most difficult part of a house to
keep dry is where the roof meets the gable-end. Not having

a long slab of stone to stretch the full length, he works with smaller, squared stones, each supporting its own weight.

'Lums' are set in the end of the house, because the fire is no longer in the middle of the room. The roofs are gay with red tiles imported from Holland, although some of the houses are covered with thatch.

Sir George Bruce is the driving force in the burgh. He has bought up most of the works for salt-making, an industry which needs a great deal of coal. He has a coal-mine which is one of the marvels of Scotland, for the coal is cut under the sea. The miners can enter the mine either by land or by sea, where a round stone tower reaching high above the water has been constructed out in the Forth. Protected from the sea by this wall of stone, they have dug down through solid rock until they reached a rich seam of coal. Piercing into it, they have cut a tunnel arched overhead and high enough for a man to stand up in. Side-cuttings branch out like side streets and closes from a main street, and

> There young and old, with glim'ring candles burning
> Digge, delve and labour.[1]

Water seeps through the roof and makes the mine wet. Three horses work a chain of buckets which bring the water to the surface and pour it back into the sea.

Along the shore, sea-water is trapped in ponds at high tide. Some of the water evaporates in the heat of the sun. Poured into rows of pans in the salt-houses, it is heated over coal fires. Steam belches forth until all the water has boiled away. The salt is shovelled into baskets and carted off to storehouses to be ready for export. Bruce's workers are now producing over ninety tons of salt a week.

Coal and salt, land and trade make Sir George Bruce rich. The miners and salters are his serfs. They have not become free like most townsmen and peasants. Wives and sons follow the men down the mine. No member of the family can escape to another trade.[2]

[1] John Taylor: *The Pennyles Pilgrimage* (1618).
[2] Miners were a class apart, and did not gain their freedom until 1799.

Mining and salt-manufacture are not the burgh's only industries. The smiths of Culross are famous for making girdles; indeed, they claim to have the monopoly of making them in Scotland. To have 'a guid Culross griddle' is the wish of every Scottish housewife as she bakes her oatmeal bannocks on the fire. Some craftsmen, like the tanners who work on skins and leather, the shoemakers, and the weavers, sell their wares in the weekly market by the Mercat Cross.

BAKING ON A GIRDLE

A man is being hustled up the steps of the Town House, charged with owing money. Behind him rushes a merchant, excited and complaining, 'I sold him a fine pair of breeks last week and he hasn't paid me a penny.'

'Save your breath for the Council,' commands the bailie who made the arrest. The case is heard by the Council and the man, found guilty, is locked in the debtor's room. If he had been guilty of any other crime he would have been put in the prison below the council chamber. When he does not reappear along with the Council, the people know that this is another case of a man who has not paid his debts. The excitement dies down. Business continues in front of the Town House at the Tron where goods are being weighed.

Not far from the Town House is Sir George Bruce's home, the finest dwelling in Culross. The house, which he modestly calls 'The Collier's House', is the sign and result of his prosperity. A big house, it has doubled in size during his lifetime. An old mason is busy chiselling the owner's initials, 'G.B.', on a stone for the top of a dormer window. Glaziers are preparing lattice windows, fitting the diamond-shaped glass together with strips of lead. The windows are not made to open and shut, but below the glass part of each window are two little doors which open to let in the air. We hear that Sir George Bruce plans to employ an artist to paint Biblical scenes on the ceilings.

Down in the harbour, men are loading cartloads of coals on board ships bound for the staple port of *Campvere* in Holland. A carter has just arrived with a load of linen yarn and bales of cloth from Dunfermline, and will carry back some wooden battens just unloaded from Norway.

Scottish Trade and Manufactures

Scotland's trade with Europe was valuable to her in the first half of the seventeenth century. Linen and woollen cloth, salt herrings, and salmon, were exported to Germany, France, and Holland. Many Scottish traders lived abroad. A Culross man—Kenorick by name—was a burgess of Danzig, and many Scotsmen were pedlars in Poland. The Scots traded most with Holland, and, at their headquarters at Campvere, they had better trading privileges than they were allowed with England. Many Scottish families settled in Campvere, where they had their own lodging house for visiting merchants and worshipped in their own church. Later, the export of coal to Holland became more important than all the trade in other goods put together.

Most of the weapons used by the Covenanters came from Holland. In 1640 and 1641, Thomas Cunningham, a merchant in Campvere, sent to Leith a frigate with twelve brass cannon, twenty tons of cannon-balls, seven thousand swords, fifteen thousand muskets, and forty-two tons of gunpowder—enough to equip a formidable army.

F

It was not through lack of encouragement or effort that trade declined later in the century. In 1681, the merchants of Edinburgh formed themselves into the Merchant Company. At the same time, Parliament passed an act forbidding the import of all kinds of cloth from abroad. Some fifty businesses were started, not only to make cloth but also to produce soap, sugar, gunpowder, and pottery, and to develop the ship-building and fishing industries of the country. One of these new enterprises was the New Mills Company near Hadding-ton. Foreign weavers came over to teach the Scots, and ships brought fine wool from Spain. Dyed wool steamed in the vats, women spun yarn, some men worked hand-looms while others finished and pressed the cloth. The place became a hive of industry. The enterprise prospered until 1707, when the Union with England allowed better quality cloth to be brought in freely from the south. The New Mills could not compete, and had to close down.

Something for You to Do

1. (a) What were the main exports from Culross?
   (b) Why did Scottish trade with Europe decay later in the century?
2. Make a list, or a set of drawings, of the features of a house in a seventeenth-century burgh. There may be some houses near you which are of this period—e.g. Gladstone's Land and many others in the Royal Mile in Edinburgh, and Provand's Lordship in Glasgow. Look out for houses with small windows, crow-stepped gables, etc.
3. What powers did a town council possess in the seventeenth century which it does not have now?
4. Try to find out if your town or neighbouring towns were founded at this time.

Chapter 27

THE UNION OF SCOTLAND AND ENGLAND

In 1690, the Scottish Parliament became free from the king's control. At last, it could take steps for the benefit of the Scottish people, steps which might not be in the best interests of England.

The Scots had one constant grievance against the English. Compared with her southern neighbour, Scotland was a poor country with no colonies and little trade. Yet, in spite of the Union of the Crowns, Scotland was considered to be a foreign country in matters of trade. She was not allowed free trade either with England or with the English colonies. In the seventeenth century, countries tried to produce all they needed for themselves, and kept out foreign goods by putting heavy duties on them. If they had colonies abroad, they reserved the colonial trade for themselves.

The Darien Scheme

Some Scottish merchants wanted to start a colony of their own, which would make money for them and for the country. William Paterson had a plan, and they thought he ought to know all about making money, as he had just helped to found the Bank of England. In 1695 they formed the 'Company of Scotland Trading to Africa and the Indies', and were given full authority to trade between Scotland and America, Africa, and Asia, for thirty-one years. People in the Lowlands invested their savings—£200,000 in all—in the new venture. *Darien*, on the narrow strip of land joining North and South America, was chosen by Paterson to become a great centre of buying and selling controlled by the Scots.

Paterson had not considered all the problems involved in establishing a colony there—the heat, malaria, the need to

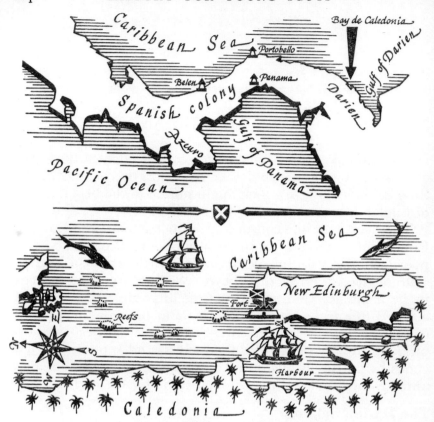

THE SITE OF THE DARIEN SCHEME

prepare the soil for cultivation or to send adequate cargoes of food. Not enough thought was given to the kinds of goods which would sell there, and certainly there was little demand for the heavy cloths, stockings, and wigs in their cargoes. The Spaniards who had settled in Central America refused to allow any other country to share in their trade. The Scots turned to the English in Jamaica for help, and were astounded when it was not given. But why, after all, should the English help Scotsmen to establish a colony which would compete with their own trade? At the time, William III hoped to keep Spain friendly, and the Scottish scheme was interfering with his plans.

The Darien Scheme was a dismal failure. Hundreds of lives were lost, and the money was gone. Illogically, the Scots in their misery put the blame not on their own mistakes and inexperience but on the king and the English merchants. The Union of the Crowns was never nearer to breaking point.

The Massacre of Glencoe

The Highlanders already had reason to hate the king. To insure against further rebellion after the battle of Killiecrankie, their chiefs were required to swear an oath of loyalty to the Crown. The deadline was the 31st December 1691. To some of the chiefs, it was a matter of honour to be slow in complying with the order. MacIan, chief of the MacDonalds of Glencoe, reported in time to the commander of the garrison at Fort William, who told him that he must go to Inveraray to take the oath before the sheriff. MacIan was old, the weather was miserable, and he struggled through the snow to Inveraray. He had to wait until the sheriff arrived, and he took the oath on the 6th January 1692. The sheriff seemed satisfied, and the old chief thought his duty done.

Sir John Dalrymple, the Master of Stair, who had the chief power in Scotland, was delighted when he heard that the McDonalds were late. Here was a chance to teach the Highlanders a lesson. A hundred and twenty soldiers, led by Campbell of Glenlyon, a deadly enemy of the MacDonalds, arrived in the glen. They came in peace, they said, and were kindly treated at the tables and firesides of the MacDonalds for nearly a fortnight. Before light one February morning, they struck. The chief was shot in his bed, and nearly forty men, women, and children were put to the sword, while others struggled through the snow to safety among the Stewarts of Appin.

Who was responsible for the 'Massacre'? Was it Dalrymple, the Master of Stair? Was he the planner or the faithful royal servant? Was it the king? He signed the order, but did he understand what was to happen? One thing is certain: the massacre made the Highlands hostile to 'Dutch William' and his government.

'The Ill Years'

From 1696 onwards the crops failed, and the people called that time 'the seven ill years'. Harvests were so late that harvesting was still going on in January. Food was dear, and people died from cold and hunger. An eye-witness tells us, 'I have seen when meal was all sold in markets, women clapping their hands and tearing the clothes off their heads, crying "How shall we go home and see our children die in hunger? They have got no meat these two days and we have nothing to give them".'

The tragedies of Glencoe, Darien, and 'the ill years', made the Scots conscious of their misery. Would it not be better to break off all connection with England and become a separate nation again? Britain was at war with France during Queen Anne's reign, and the English, fearing that the Scots might select a king of their own and revive the 'Auld Alliance' with France, decided to allow the Scots free trade, if they would consent to the creation of a British Parliament.

Queen Anne

The Act of Union

In 1707 this closer union, the Union of the Parliaments, took place. It meant the end of the old Scottish Parliament, where lords, lairds, and burgesses had all sat in the same House and, as Andrew Fairservice said in *Rob Roy*, 'didna' need to hae the same blethers twice ower'. Forty-five Members of Parliament were to represent Scotland in the British House of Commons, and the Scottish lords were to choose sixteen of their number to sit in the House of Lords.

English and colonial markets were open to Scottish merchants. At first, Scottish manufactures could not compare

with English ones, but increasing numbers of cattle were
driven into England along the tracks used by Border raiders
for centuries past. The cattle trade brought a welcome
return in cash, which was used to develop agriculture and
the linen industry. Glasgow merchants soon shared in the
import of tobacco from Virginia, and the town prospered.

Both countries adopted the same coins, weights and
measures, and their Union was marked by a new flag,
blending the crosses of St. George and St. Andrew. They

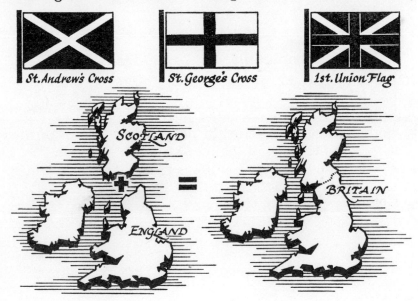

St. Andrew's Cross St. George's Cross 1st. Union Flag

agreed to the succession of the Protestant house of Hanover
on the death of Queen Anne, but in religion and law Scotland
clung to her old ways. The Presbyterian Kirk remained the
established Church in Scotland. Her system of law is
different from English law. For instance, an English jury
must be unanimous, whereas in Scotland a majority verdict
is sufficient. Again, in England a prisoner is found either
'guilty' or 'not guilty', while in Scotland a third verdict of
'not proven' may be brought in.

The two peoples united to form one country, Great Britain.
Their history as separate countries came to an end. After

1707, their politics and relations with other countries became the subject-matter of British history. This does not mean that the Scottish nation ceased to exist. Scotland has its own local dialects, songs, dances, stories, customs, and traditions—everything that makes up Scottish culture and makes us feel 'Scottish'. The feeling of nationality is still strong. If you attend an international rugby or football match, you will realise that the attachment of Scottish people to their team, and therefore to the country it represents, is not dead.

Something for You to Do

1. Write an account of the Massacre of Glencoe as if you had been an eye-witness.
2. Why did the Darien Scheme fail?
3. Copy out the main terms of the Act of Union. Add the date, and the name of the monarch who signed it.
4. Has Scotland benefited by union with England? Discuss this question in class.
5. Complete your time chart.

INDEX

(Italics signify names of battles)

Time Chart

Ancient Civilizations

4,000 B.C.

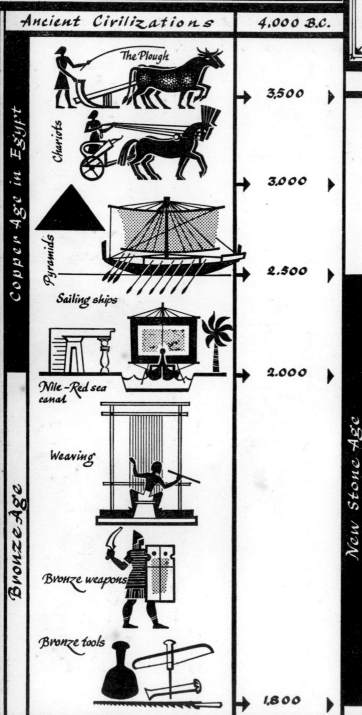

Copper Age in Egypt

The Plough

Chariots

Pyramids

Sailing ships

Nile–Red sea canal

3,500

3,000

2,500

2,000

No human beings

Beachcombers

Hunters

Bronze Age

Weaving

Bronze weapons

Bronze tools

1,800

New Stone Age

Herdsmen

Farmers

Maeshowe